RHUBARBARIA

For Joan Thirsk and Ann Prior

RHUBARBARIA

RECIPES FOR RHUBARB

MARY PRIOR

PROSPECT BOOKS

2009

First published in 2009 by Prospect Books,
Allaleigh House, Blackawton, Totnes, Devon TQ9 7DL.

British Library Cataloguing in Publication Data:
A catalogue entry for this book is available from the British
Library.

ISBN 978-1-903018-61-3

Typeset by Tom Jaine.

Printed and bound in Malta by Gutenberg Press Ltd.

Mixed Sources
Product group from well-managed
forests, and other controlled sources
www.fsc.org Cert no. TT-CoC-002424
© 1996 Forest Stewardship Council

The paper used for this book is FSC-certified and
totally chlorine-free. FSC (the Forest Stewardship
Council) is an international network to promote
responsible management of the world's forests.

CONTENTS

ACKNOWLEDGEMENTS

I acknowledge with great pleasure and warmest thanks the debt I owe many writers and cooks whose recipes and comments on rhubarb have instructed and inspired me. Their books are listed in the bibliography and often referred to in the text. I must record my indebtedness to various contributors to the little booklets of recipes sold by the women of various churches and women's guilds. I am also grateful to Sally Butcher, Philippa Davenport, Christine France, Joyce Molyneux and Helen Saberi who have allowed their published recipes to figure in the text and to Gillian Riley for permission to print her translation of Giacomo Castelvetro.

A recipe for rhubarb wine appeared in *The Orcadian*, and was sent me by Frances Pelly. Other recipes were sent by Andrina Teed and Kristin Pétersdóttir. Still more were given me by friends in Shetland: Anne Sinclair, Stella Sutherland, Ingirid Eunson, Rosa Steppanova and the late Anna Smith; in England: the late Mrs E. A. Davies; in New Zealand: Helen Leach and Mavis Oddie; and in Tokyo: Susan Ugawa. In England I was helped and encouraged in a variety of ways by Martin and Joanna Dodsworth and Christine Holmes. Brian Smith and Angus Johnson at the Shetland Archives have found me many references, while the staff of the Bodleian Library Upper Reserve have been extremely helpful. John Whitwell, director of the Stockbridge House Experimental Horticultural Station at Cawood showed me the great variety of rhubarb growing there and introduced me to growers. That was in 1985, before the National Collection was moved to Harrogate. Jeremy Godwin, in a letter full of recipes, gave me the title for the book. Joan Thirsk and Anne Lawrence vetted the manuscript, while my daughter gave me recipes and advice and word-processed the manuscript. Finally, I would like to thank Tom Jaine for his tactful editing and contributions to the text which have greatly improved the whole.

Mary Prior
Oxford, 2009

PREFACE

Rhubarb is a word which rolls on the tongue with relish. It sounds both rude and absurd, and the imagination has found all sorts of uses for it, many listed in Partridge's *Dictionary of Slang*. It is uttered by actors in crowd scenes, and the action is called rhubarbing. It means a rumpus or a nonsense – as in 'that's a load of rhubarb'. In low-life it means the genitals. In Scots, to 'gie somebody rhubarb' is to beat them up. Whether these associations gathered around the word first, and slowly brought obloquy to the poor innocent plant or vice versa is a byway in the history of fashion which is unexplored. I hope this little book will rehabilitate the plant. Not much can be done about its literary associates.

None of these associations of the word was known in our family – a rather sheltered environment – though rhubarb itself played an important part in the family economy. I grew up in New Zealand in the 1930s, a 'daughter of the Manse', with all its connotations of Scottish Presbyterianism. It was a busy, hospitable household, with much coming and going: members of the congregation, ministers and elders from country parishes up for Presbytery, students, members of committees, Bible Class girls, missionaries, uncles, cousins and aunts. My mother had an almost superstitious belief in the importance of 'breaking bread together' in bonding people and solving their problems. In her eyes Judas Iscariot and the Campbells were about equal in betraying the bonds that breaking bread created. None escaped without a cup of tea and a scone, many stayed for dinner. When there were more guests than my mother's optimistic view of the contents of the safe could satisfy, I would be sent down the garden to pick rhubarb – a trip made memorable by the fear that my sister's vicious bantam rooster might have escaped, and be lurking in the rhubarb patch.

I don't think we ever did anything with it but stew it and serve it with custard or curds and cream, but on very special occasions the ginger jar would appear and preserved ginger and syrup made it a feast. It would be too much to say of it that it was 'an ever-present aid in time of trouble', but it was certainly an 'ever-present aid'.

Years later in Oxford, in the early days of widowhood, I rediscovered rhubarb. I became an allotment-holder, and found it growing freely around many disused plots. I was not a successful gardener. Twitch and convolvulus played their part, but I certainly ate more of this rhubarb than of my own produce. However, when I gave up the allotment I planted a couple of Timperley Earlys in my garden and began trying out rhubarb recipes. Superior recipe books barely mentioned it, but my 1947 edition of *Farmhouse Fare*, drawing on the recipes of country housewives collected by the *Farmers' Weekly*, had more than a dozen recipes for puddings alone; almost as many as for apples, more than for gooseberries or plums, whose seasons are shorter. It arrived as the country housewife's last apples were beginning to rot and lasted into the season of small fruits, seeing her through the long gap when no other seasonal fruits were available.

Some years later again, on holiday in Shetland, I saw it growing in every garden, and around old abandoned crofts. It grew with an uninhibited luxuriance, indeed, far better than anything else in those windswept islands, and it formed an important item in the Shetland diet. Where did it come from, how did it reach these isolated islands? Or was it a native? Was this where all the world's rhubarb came from?

It was not, and is not. Its history is much more extraordinary. It was known first in the Western world as a dried root, a valuable drug which came from the East, but how far east, no-one knew. I shall very briefly trace its history from its use as a drug to its rise as a culinary plant, once fashionable, later a Cinderella of the dinner table, despised by generations of schoolchildren. It is, however, a chameleon of the food world, combining and contrasting with a wide range of exotic and homely ingredients to yield many happy surprises.

The larger part of this book consists, though, of an anthology of recipes. They are drawn from a wide variety of sources, from the writings of professional cooks to collections of recipes put together for good causes, manuscript recipe books and letters, and a few of my own, and those of my friends.

Rhubarb was fashionable in the early nineteenth century, when it was still a novelty, and recently, with increasing interest in seasonal food, it has become fashionable again. In the early spring the glossies provide wonderful party dishes by our best traditional cooks with the minutest directions which, if followed exactly, guarantee success. Not all of us have, however, the right sized baking pans and pie dishes, ovens whose temperature is reliable, or families of the stipulated size. We live in an imperfect world, and we have to alter recipes to suit the world we live in. But remember if you use good ingredients, even if you fail to produce the dish of your dreams, unless you have burnt it to a cinder, it will almost certainly taste wonderful, and may even open your eyes to new possibilities. I remember the cake in which the rhubarb never really cooked, from which I learnt the pleasure of rhubarb *al dente*. The cake was made in the wrong sized tin and more or less fell out on to the cake plate in a blowzy sort of way. It was a big cake and there were only two of us, but it never stood a chance.

Rhubarb provides enormous possibilities to the adventurous cook: to those who find exhilaration in cooking well with what comes to hand, I hope this book will provide the wherewithal for further explorations of their own.

RHUBARB IN BRITAIN

As familiar as rhubarb may be to generations of Britons, it is a johnny-come-lately to the garden and table. We have been eating it for no more than two centuries, but for much, much longer we have been taking it as medicine. Its history, therefore, can sometimes be muddling and as a first step to sorting it out, I have laid out the essence of the article on the plant printed in volume 23 of the 1911 edition of the *Encyclopædia Britannica*.

RHUBARB.
The name is applied both to a drug and a vegetable.

The drug has been used in medicine from very early times, being described in the Chinese herbal *Pen-king*, which is believed to date from 2700 BC. The name seems to be a corruption of *Rheum barbarum* or *Reu barbarum*, a designation applied to the drug as early as the middle of the 6th century, and apparently identical with the ρηον or ρα of Dioscorides, described by him as a root brought from beyond the Bosporus. In the 14th century rhubarb appears to have found its way to Europe by way of the Indus and Persian Gulf to the Red Sea and Alexandria, and was therefore described at "East Indian" rhubarb. Some also came by way of Persia and the Caspian to Syria and Asia Minor, and reached Europe from the ports of Aleppo and Smyrna, and became known as "Turkey" rhubarb. Subsequently to the year 1653, when China first permitted Russia to trade on her frontiers, Chinese rhubarb reached Europe chiefly by way of Moscow; and in 1704 the rhubarb trade became a monopoly of the Russian government, in consequence of which the term "Russian" or "crown" rhubarb came to be applied to it. Urga was the great depot for the rhubarb trade in 1719, but in 1728 the depot was transferred to Kiachta. All rhubarb brought to the depot passed through the hands of the government inspector; hence Russian rhubarb was invariably good and obtained a remarkably high price. This severe supervision naturally led, as soon as the northern Chinese ports were thrown open to European trade, to a new outlet being sought; and the increased demand for the drug at these ports resulted in less care being exercised by the Chinese in the collection and curing of the root, so that the rhubarb of good quality offered at Kiachta rapidly dwindled in quantity, and after 1860 Russian rhubarb ceased to appear in European commerce. Owing to the expense of carrying the drug across the whole breadth of Asia, and the difficulty of preserving it from the attacks of insects, rhubarb was formerly one of the most costly of drugs. In 1542 it was sold in France for ten times the price of cinnamon and four times that of saffron, and in an English price list bearing the date of 1657 it is quoted at 16s. per lb, opium being at that time only 6s. and scammony 12s. per lb.

...The botanical source of Chinese rhubarb cannot be said to have been as yet definitely cleared up by the actual identification of plants to be used for the purpose. *Rheum palmatum, R. officinale, R. palmatum*, var. *tanguticum, R. colinianum* and *R. Franzenbachii* have been variously stated to be the source of it, but the roots produced by these species under cultivation in Europe do not present the characteristic network of white veins exhibited by the best specimens of the Chinese drug.

...The most important constituent of this drug, giving it its purgative properties and its yellow colour, is chrysarobin.... The rhubarb of commerce also contains chrysophanic acid, a dioxymethyl anthraquinone ... of which chrysarobin is a reduction product.

...Rhubarb is produced in the four northern provinces

of China proper (Chih-li, Shan-se, Shen-se and Ho-nan), in the north-west provinces of Kan-suh, formerly included in Shen-se, but now extending across the desert of Gobi to the frontier of Tibet, in the Mongolian province of Tsing-hai, including the salt lake Koko-nor, and the districts of Tangut, Sifan and Turfan, and in the mountains of the western provinces of Sze-chuen. Two of the most important centres of the trade are Sining-fu in the province of Kan-suh, and Kwanhien in Sze-chuen. From Shen-se, Kan-suh and Sze-chuen the rhubarb is forwarded to Hankow, and thence carried to Shanghai, whence it is shipped to Europe. Lesser quantities are shipped from Tien-tsin, and occasionally the drug is exported from Canton, Amoy, Fuh-chow and Ning-po.

Very little is known concerning the mode of preparing the drug for the market. According to Mr Bell, who on a journey from St Petersburg to Peking had the opportunity of observing the plant in a growing state, the root is not considered to be mature until it is six years old. It is then dug up, usually in the autumn, and deprived of its cortical portion and the smaller branches, and the larger pieces are divided in half longitudinally; these pieces are bored with holes and strung up on cords to dry, in some cases being previously subjected to a preliminary drying on stone slabs heated by fire underneath. In Bhutan the root is said to be hung up in a kind of drying room, in which a moderate heat is regularly maintained. The effect produced by the two drying processes is very different: when dried by artificial heat, the exterior of the pieces becomes hardened before the interior has entirely lost its moisture, and consequently the pieces decay in the centre, although the surface may show no change. These two varieties are technically known as kiln-dried and sun-dried; and it was on account of this difference in quality that the Russian officer at Kiachta had every piece examined by boring a hole to its centre.

...As early as 1608 Prosper Alpinus of Padua cultivated as the true rhubarb a plant that is now known as *Rheum rhaponticum*, a native of southern Siberia and the basin of the Volga. This plant was introduced into England through Sir Matthew Lister, physician to Charles I, who gave the seed obtained by him in Italy to the botanist Parkinson. The culture of this rhubarb for the sake of the root was commenced in 1777 at Banbury, in Oxfordshire, by an apothecary named Hayward, the plants being raised from seed sent from Russia in 1762, and with such success that the Society of Arts awarded him a silver medal in 1789 and a gold one in 1794. The cultivation subsequently extended to Somersetshire, Yorkshire and Middlesex, but it is now chiefly carried on at Banbury. English rhubarb root is sold at a cheaper rate than the Chinese rhubarb, and forms a considerable article of export to America, and is said to be used in Britain in the form of powder which is of a finer yellow colour than that of Chinese rhubarb. The Banbury rhubarb appears to be a hybrid between *R. rhaponticum* and *R. undulatum* – the root, according to E. Colin, not presenting the typical microscopic structure of the former. More recently, good rhubarb has been grown at Banbury from *Rheum officinale*, but these two varieties are not equal in medicinal strength to the Chinese article.... In France, the cultivation of rhubarb was commenced in the latter half of the 18th century – *R. compactum*, *R. palmatum*, *R. rhaponticum* and *R. undulatum* being the species grown. The cultivation has, however, now nearly ceased, small quantities only being prepared at Avignon and a few other localities.

The cultivation of *Rheum compactum* was begun in Moravia in the beginning of the present century by Prikyl, an apothecary in Austerlitz, and until about fifty years ago the root was largely exported to Lyons and Milan, where it was used for dyeing silk. As a medicine 5 parts are stated to be equal to 4 of Chinese rhubarb. Rhubarb root is also grown at Auspitz in Moravia and at Ilmitz, Kremnitz and Frauenkirchen in Hungary; *R. emodi* is said to be cultivated for the same purpose in Silesia.

Rhubarb is also prepared for use in medicine from wild species in the Himalayas and Java.

The rhubarb used as a vegetable consists of the leaf stalks of *R. rhaponticum* and its varieties, and *R. undulatum*. It is known in America as pie-plant. Plants are readily raised from seed, but strong plants can be obtained in a much shorter time by dividing the roots. Divisions or seedlings are planted about 3 ft. apart in ground which has been deeply trenched and manured, the crowns being kept slightly above the surface. Rhubarb grows freely under fruit-trees, but succeeds best in an open situation in rich, rather light soil. The stalks should not be pulled during the first season. If a top-dressing of manure be given each winter a plantation will last good for several years. Forced rhubarb is much esteemed in winter and early spring, and forms a remunerative crop. Forcing under glass or in a mushroom house is most satisfactory, but open-ground forcing may be effected by placing pots or boxes over the roots and burying in a good depth of stable litter and leaves. Several other species, such a *R. palmatum*, *R. officinale*, *R. nobile* and others, are cultivated for their fine foliage and handsome inflorescence, especially in wild gardens, margins of shrubberies and similar places. They succeed in most soils, but prefer a rich soil of good depth. They are propagated by seeds or by division.

All the chief facts of the plant's history are touched on here. Known to the ancients in both China and the Mediterranean, it was valued as a remedy for a costive digestion, a purgative. And the useful part of the plant was not its stalk but its root. Most likely, the Greek physician Dioscorides (who flourished in Cilicia in the first century AD) obtained his supplies from regions to the east of the Black Sea rather than far-away China. The name rhubarb itself combines two elements: *rheon* or *rha* denoting the Volga basin, and *barbarum* referring to the barbarians who lived thereabouts. Species of rhubarb grew throughout central Asia, as far north as Siberia, but the Chinese root would be the most important, if only because the most efficacious. As a general rule, this Chinese medicinal rhubarb was *Rheum palmatum* and its cousins, while the early rhubarb grown closer to our European home was *R. rhaponticum* or *R. rhabarbarum*. This latter was smaller than the Chinese varieties, more stalky, less rooty. It is also important to stress, in the light of later botanical explorations and hypotheses, that rhubarb does not breed true from seed. The traffic in seeds, therefore, will often throw up false trails and anomalies.

That medical aspect of the plant need not detain us over-long. Its ramifications are detailed with affectionate brio by Professor Clifford M. Foust in his *Rhubarb: The Wondrous Drug*, published in 1992. But it is worth emphasizing that it was held in almost universal esteem in early-modern Europe and that it survives even today as the active ingredient of many Italian digestive bitters. An early reference to how it hit the spot is found in the Italian exile Giacomo Castelvetro's account of the greenstuffs of his homeland, dedicated in 1614 to Lucy, Countess of Bedford. By his lights, the cure he recounts was effected by raisins, but we know better: it was the powdered rhubarb.

> I was once living in the neighbourhood of San Grigioni, in the small but pleasant village of Piuri, a mile and a half from the rather larger town of Chiavenna, when I was taken ill with a serious and dangerous affliction, an unbelievably unpleasant attack of constipation. It was

so bad that I went for ten or eleven days without relief, which when it came caused such intense pain that I do not believe a woman in childbirth could have suffered more than I. In this sorry state, hoping that God in His mercy might cure me, I took myself off on some errand or other to Chiavenna. When I got there I went straight to the pharmacy of Francesco Bottighisio of Bergamo. (This distinguished man was obliged to live in exile there because of his religious views.)

He greeted me affectionately and asked me kindly how I came to be so yellow and bloated, and when he heard about my affliction, smiled and said: 'There's no question but that with God's help I shall soon be able to clear this up for you; come back tomorrow for something I shall have got ready for you.' So I thanked him and went back to Piuri, and returned the next day to find that he had prepared a medicine for me in the following way: Take one ounce of raisins and soak them in dry, not sweet, malmsey. Drain them in a sieve, and when they have dried a little, mix them with a dram of powdered rhubarb.

I was to take some of these raisins when I got up in the morning and walk up and down the room chewing them, before swallowing them. This I did straight away, and after only one or two doses, I was completely cured of my unpleasant affliction. Ever since then, and that was over forty years ago, I have never been constipated for more than two or three days without relief.

That is all I have to say about this remedy, except that the dose is a spoonful, and that if I don't have any malmsey, I use a good white wine instead. I have, to my credit, used this medicine to help many a sufferer.

(Translated from the Italian by Gillian Riley.)

Doubtless the sweet raisins helped the rhubarbaric medicine go down. The pre-eminence of this sovereign remedy can be gauged from the diaries of the Reverend James Woodforde, living in Norfolk in the last quarter of the eighteenth century. Whatever the ailment, the root was pressed into service. 'Briton [his servant] very poorly today, a violent purging which he is subject to some times. I gave him some Rhubarb, going to bed', he wrote in 1797. 'My Servant Man poorly this Afternoon. My Servant Maid very bad in a cold, coughed very Much to day, obliged to go to bed early to night. I gave them both at going to bed, a small dose of Rhubarb', was an entry in 1802. Parson Woodforde also supplies us with an early reference to eating rhubarb tarts. In 1793, after a busy day visiting friends and colleagues, he had for dinner, 'hashed Calfs Head and a fore Quarter of Lamb rosted & a Rhubarb Tart.'

The cultivation of rhubarb in the British Isles and the near Continent was at first bound up with this medicinal use. As noted above, the Chinese root was exceedingly dear. When the fashion for the remedy increased (and purgatives and cathartics were among the most important weapons in any apothecary's armoury, second only, perhaps, to quinine or Peruvian bark) so did the potential for a financial bonanza to whomever succeeded in first discovering, then growing the genuine plant closer to home. Eventually, people were convinced they had the original Chinese rhubarb and many efforts were made to develop a domestic industry, particularly by the Hayward family near Banbury and by the Superintendent of the Royal Botanic Garden in Edinburgh, Professor John Hope. People may have pursued its cultivation as an 'alternative' agricultural product; the Duke of Atholl, for example, had a large plantation at Blair Castle in Perthshire which he sold to an Edinburgh druggist (C. Anne Wilson, 1973). But the effective strength of any European root never matched that from China. Production continued, as did export of the medicine to the New World, but great wealth was not the consequence.

As they attempted to discover the true Chinese rhubarb, explorers and travellers, doctors and botanists combined in a delightful virtual republic that stretched across the European worlds, exchanging seeds, reporting discoveries and suggesting alternatives. Some early seeds of R. *rhaponticum* (which was never the genuine Chinese article) came to England in the sixteenth and seventeenth centuries. The first importation was possibly by the physician, former Carthusian monk, traveller and ambassador at large Andrew Boorde who wrote in 1535 to Henry VIII's secretary of state Thomas Cromwell that he had 'sentt to your mastershepp the seedes of reuberbe, the which come owtt off barbary.' What happened to these, no-one knows, and we had to wait until the contact of Sir Matthew Lister with the botanic garden in Padua during the next century before serious experiments could begin, mostly by the pioneering gardener and apothecary John Parkinson in his garden in Long Acre.

Matters got more exciting in the eighteenth century when travellers to Russia and beyond began to bring back news and specimens of more exotic varieties of the plant (much more likely to be the real thing), especially R. *undulatum* and R. *palmatum*. One of the earliest of these was John Bell of Antermony, a Scots physician who, like many of his countrymen, sought his fortune in Russia during the reign of Peter the Great. Bell was appointed physician to a Russian Embassy to China. On his journey he made an interesting observation:

I should not have mentioned an animal as well known as the marmot had it not been on account of the rhubarb. Where you see ten or twenty plants growing, you are sure of finding several burrows under the shades of their broad spreading leaves. Perhaps they may sometimes eat the leaves and roots of this plant. However, it is probable the manure they leave about the roots, contributes not a little to its increase ... it grows in tufts, at uncertain distances, as if the seeds had been dropped by design... and should it fall among the loose earth thrown up by the marmots, it immediately takes root, and produces a new plant.

Professor Foust thought Bell did not collect any seed. However, he was mistaken. Bell's account of his travels came out in 1763, and when in 1765 Professor John Hope, of the Royal Physic Garden in Edinburgh, wrote to congratulate him on his description of the true rhubarb, Bell wrote in reply,

In my return from China I brought some seeds home and sowed them in a pot ... [which were] afterwards transplanted into a border and prospered wonderfully. Last spring having occasion to make some alterations to my Garden, I removed the whole plant & was surprised to find such large roots, I dare say they weighed 7. or 8. lb. Weight ... I made no draft of the plant, nor have I seen any, neither have I seen any plant in Europe, save those at St. Petersburg, & 2. or 3. which I have spared to my friends. Mr. Miller of Chelsea told me he had sowed the seed more than once, but they never came up.

Bell returned from China about 1722 or 1723. His rhubarb had plenty of time to develop large roots by the time he dug it up – whenever that was. The Miller mentioned in his letter was Philip Miller, chief gardener at the Chelsea Physic Garden from 1722 and author of the most important eighteenth-century gardening book, *The Gardener's Dictionary* (1731). The mention given to rhubarb in this work would seem to confirm his failure to cultivate the new *R. undulatum* sent him by John Bell and shows the botanical muddle that surrounded the species. *Lapathum*, his name for the dock family with which he groups rhubarb, is nowadays more usually *Rumex*.

LAPATHUM, [takes its Name of the Greek word λαπαζω to *evacuate*, because the Root of this Plant purges the Belly: One Species of it is call'd *Hippolapathum*, of ιππος an *Horse*; and λαπαθον, as much as to say *Great Lapathum*: and another is call'd Patience, of its gentle Virtue; and *Rhabarbarum Monachorum*, i.e. *Monks Rhubarb.*] The Dock.

The *Characters* are;

The Cup of the Flower consists of six Leaves, three of which are large, and of a red Colour; the other three are lesser, and green: In the middle of the Cup are placed six Stamina: The three outer small Leaves of the Cup fall away when ripe; but the three inner large Leaves join together, and form a triangular Covering, in the middle of which are contain'd shining three-corner'd Seeds.

There are great Varieties of these Plants, which are preserv'd in some Gardens, to increase their Number: but as many of them are very common in *England*, and, if transplanted into a good Garden, and permitted to scatter their Seeds, do become very troublesome Weeds; so I shall only name two or three of the most valuable Sorts in this Place.

1. LAPATHUM; *praestantissimum, Rhubarbarum officinarum dictum. Mor. Hist.* The Pontick Rhubarb.

2. LAPATHUM; *Alpinum, folio subrotundo. Mor. Hist.* Round-leav'd Alpine Dock, *by some call'd* Monks Rhubarb.

3. LAPATHUM; *hortense, folio oblongo, sive secundum Dioscoridis. C.B.P.* Long-leav'd Garden Dock, *or* Patience.

The first of the Plants is by some suppos'd to be the true *Rhubarb*. But that does not appear, from the Figure and Consistence of the Roots, which in this plant, however cultivated with us, is not of the same Colour; nor has it such a Resin as is found in the true; and the Shape of the Roots appear very different, as is also the Strength in Medicine: so that until the true *Rhubarb* is better known, there can little be said with Certainty on this Head.

The second Sort is sometimes cultivated in Gardens, for Medicinal Use; tho' there is a Dispute whether this be the true *Monks Rhubarb* or not: but there is no great difference between the Roots of this Plant, and the other disputed Sort; so that either may be indifferently used.

The third Sort was formerly cultivated in Gardens as a Pot-herb; but of late Years it has been wholly disus'd for that Purpose, and now only preserv'd in Gardens for Medicinal Use.

These Plants are all easily propagated by sowing their Seeds in *Autumn*, soon after they are ripe, or early the succeeding *Spring*, in a rich, light, moist Soil, where they will grow to be very large, and, if singled out to the Distance of three Feet, will produce large strong Roots, which will be fit for Use the second Year after sowing; when they should be taken up soon after the Leaves are decay'd, and dry'd in a shady Place where the Air may freely pass between them.

Note that each of the three plants he describes, rhubarb, monk's rhubarb and patience, were grown for their roots. Just as the Chinese version, they would be dried and powdered, then deployed as a mild laxative or purge.

It was a few years after he wrote this that Miller began to have more success with new supplies of *R. undulatum*, drawn mostly from contacts at the botanic gardens of St Petersburg. Another Englishman who benefited from Russian supplies of seed was Peter Collinson. He was in touch with John Bartram, at the time America's most enterprising student of these matters and he thought to send him some seeds to try in the New World. The letter announcing this is a marvellous example of the freemasonry of enthusiasts that kept the ferment of discovery and botanic innovation alive in the eighteenth century. It is worth quoting in full but its length might test the reader's patience. The text is found in Darlington 1849, pp. 133–135, and the nub of the matter is in this paragraph:

London, September 2, 1739.

Dear Friend John [Peter Collinson was a Quaker]:
I have this day received a letter from Petersburgh; and am assured, per Doctor Ammann, Professor of Botany there, that the Siberian Rhubarb is the true sort. I wish a quantity was produced with you, to try the experiment. Both this and the Rhapontic make excellent tarts, before most other fruits fit for that purpose are ripe. All you have to do, is to take the stalks from the root, and from the leaves; peel off the rind, and cut them in two or three pieces, and put them in crust with sugar and a little cinnamon; then bake the pie, or tart: eats best cold. It is much admired here, and has none of the effects that the roots have. It eats most like gooseberry pie.

This is the first mention we have of rhubarb tart in England. A printed recipe was not to appear for more than twenty years.

Before we leave these years of Georgian exploration – the necessary prelude to the arrival of rhubarb on our tables – we should mention another Scot, another doctor, who worked in Russia and returned from thence with a parcel of seed. He was James Mounsey (1709–1773), from Dumfriesshire. He served for many years in Russia, at first with the army under General Keith and later as personal physician to the Empress Elizabeth. Under her successor, Paul III, he was chief physician, privy councillor and medical director of the armed forces. When Paul was assassinated in 1762, Mounsey was dismissed by the Empress Catherine. Legend has it that the Scot was in such fear of the garrotte – after his protector's own precipitate dispatch – that he escaped the country by faking his own death. Returning to his native heath, he built a handsome residence near Lockerbie (it still survives). Each room in the house had two doors (the extra one, they say, for a hasty escape should he be set upon by assassins). He also made extensive plantations of his new rhubarb (which was *R. palmatum*) while distributing seeds to his learned acquaintance north and south of the border. Many would say that the most significant efforts to reduce the pre-eminence of China stem from this new importation. James Mounsey lives on. His ghost ('Old Jacobus') haunts the library of Rammerscales Mansion. When a teacher training college was evacuated there during the Second World War, students refused to occupy the house and slept for preference in the stables.

Perhaps they should have taken a dose of rhubarb to quiet their fluttering stomachs. These two new varieties of rhubarb, the *undulatum* and *palmatum*, were not really edible themselves, but when hybridized with the older breed *rhaponticum* (which had been growing in English gardens since those early seventeenth-century exchanges) they did offer a larger and more toothsome stalk to the cook's delight. This process of cross-breeding must have gone on through the middle of the eighteenth century, allowing the plant to be wholly domesticated by its closing years. Erasmus Darwin, father of Charles, put it succinctly (Darwin 1800, pp. 525–526):

> The *rheum hybridum*, mule rhubarb, described in Murray's *Systema Vegetabilium*, edition the fourteenth, I believe to be produced between the palmated rhubarb, and the common rhubarb of our gardens, or *rheum rhaphonticum*; as it appeared both in my garden and my neighbours amongst a mixture of those two kinds of rhubarb, without being previously placed or sown there. The leaf is very large and pointed, without being palmated, and is a week or two forwarder in the spring than either of the other rhubarbs, and the peeled stalks are asserted by connoisseurs in eating to make the best possible of all tarts, much superior to those of the palmated or rhaphontic rhubarb; and, are so much more valuable as a luxury, as they precede by a month the gooseberry and early apple; and may be well propagated by dividing the roots, as they do not produce seed in all summers.

The earliest recipe for rhubarb tart that I have so far found in an English cookery book is that by Hannah Glasse in her *Compleat Confectioner* of *c.* 1760. She is clearly aware that she is dealing with something novel. She writes, 'these tarts may be thought very odd, but they are very fine ones and have a pretty flavour.' So far as I am aware, they do not reappear in print until John Farley's *The London Art of Cookery* which first appeared in 1783. The seventh edition of 1792 says:

> *Rhubarb Tarts.*
> Take the stalks of the rubarb that grows in the garden, peel it, and cut it into the size of a gooseberry, and make it as gooseberry tart.

This instruction, which gives hardly more detail than Peter Collinson's in his letter to John Bartram, is repeated virtually word for word in the early editions of William Augustus Henderson's *The Housekeeper's Instructor* of the 1790s (save that he spells rhubarb as rheubarb). And it is the standard wording of many other tart recipes found in English cookery books of the turn of that century. It was not, however, until the first years of the following century that the trickle of suggestions grows to a flood, including tarts, pies, jams, wines and other things. Some of these pioneer recipes are reprinted in the chapters which follow.

Talking of pioneers, a cap should be doffed to that great original of Regency cooking, Dr William Kitchiner. His *Cook's Oracle* (originally *Apicius Redivivus; or, The Cook's Oracle*), first published in 1817 and repeatedly thereafter is perhaps the most entertaining and, dare I say it, most instructive of manuals of this era. His recipes regarding 'spring fruit', i.e. rhubarb, are worth quoting in full, in preference to scattering them through the relevant chapters. The text is that printed for the new edition of 1829.

TO DRESS SPRING FRUIT.

Spring Fruit Soup.

Peel and well wash four dozen sticks of Rhubarb; blanch it in water three or four minutes; drain it on a sieve, and put it into a stew-pan, with two Onions sliced, a Carrot, an ounce of lean Ham, and a good bit of Butter; let it stew gently over a slow fire till tender; then put in two quarts of good *Consommé*, to which add two or three ounces of Bread-crumbs; boil about fifteen minutes; skim off all the fat; season with salt and Cayenne pepper; pass it through a tamis, and serve up with fried bread.

Spring Fruit Pudding.

Clean as above three or four dozen sticks of Rhubarb; put it in a stew-pan, with the peel of a Lemon, a bit of Cinnamon, two Cloves, and as much moist sugar as will sweeten it; set it over a fire, and reduce it to a marmalade; pass it through a hair-sieve; then add the peel of a Lemon, and half a Nutmeg grated, a quarter of a pound of good Butter, and the yolks of four Eggs and one white, and mix all well together; line a pie-dish (that will just contain it) with good puff paste; put the mixture in, and bake it half an hour.

Spring Fruit – A Mock Gooseberry Sauce for Mackerel, &c.

Make a Marmalade of three dozen sticks of Rhubarb, sweetened with moist Sugar; pass it through a hair-sieve, and serve up in a sauce-boat.

Spring Fruit Tart.

Prepare Rhubarb as above; cut it into small pieces into a Tart-dish; sweeten with Loaf-Sugar pounded; cover it with a good short crust paste; sift a little Sugar over the top, and bake half an hour in a rather hot oven: serve up cold.

Spring Fruit Sherbet.

Boil six or eight sticks of Rhubarb (quite clean) ten minutes in a quart of water; strain the liquor through a tamis into a jug, with the peel of a lemon cut very thin, and two table-spoonsful of clarified Sugar; let it stand five or six hours, and it is fit to drink.

Most interesting is his suggestion that you should substitute gooseberry with rhubarb for a mackerel sauce. His soup, like Stephana Malcolm's spring soup in the soup chapter, but not like many of those northern European spring fruit soups, is made from savoury ingredients.

The common view is that rhubarb would never have gained culinary traction had it not been for the rapid decline in the price of sugar from the later eighteenth century. This, it's true, must have helped. But the development of more palatable hybrids must have been more significant – as was the entry of rhubarb into urban produce markets. After all, English people had been coping with the sourest of ingredients since time immemorial: barberries, green gooseberries, crab apples, various sorts of wild plum – none of these was sweetly toothsome.

Another important preliminary to the acceptance of the plant as a foodstuff was that the cook should be clear that the stalk might be edible, but the leaf was not. The oxalic acid (present in many other plants such as spinach and sorrel, even tea) contained in the broad leaves of the rhubarb was sufficient, perhaps, to kill, certainly to make unwell (the acid has most effect on the kidneys). Current American medical websites remark, 'Deaths have been reported, but are rare.' The University of Idaho reports that the death of a goat was put down to its voracious demolition of a rhubarb patch when it escaped its paddock, but goats are like that. This distinction between stalk and leaf was not always appreciated by earlier writers. Professor Foust remarks that some in the sixteenth-century suggested using rhubarb as if it were spinach or beet greens. Gerard's *Herbal* (in the 1636 edition) suggests that the leaves might be eaten like spinach, and John Parkinson wrote in 1629 that the leaves had a highly refined and acid flavour. John Gerard's grand anecdote concerning the medicinal use of the leaves is probably nearer the mark. A Maidstone surgeon had a butcher's boy with a bad case of ague. As a cure, 'he tooke out of his garden three or fower leaves of the plant of rubarbe, which myselfe had among other simples given him, which he stamped and strained with a draugt of ale, and gave it the ladde in the morning to drinke: it wrought extremely downwarde and upwarde within one hower after, and never ceassed untill night.' (As well it might.) Thomas Jefferson, when noting work done in his vegetable garden at Monticello in Virginia, remarked that in 1809 he sowed one row of *Rheum undulatum,* 'the leaves excellent as Spinach'. This misapprehension died hard. In the first edition of *Larousse Gastronomique* (1938), the editors remark that the leaves eat like spinach. Waverley Root's fine dictionary of food (1980) notes that the French *Dictionnaire de l'Académie des Gastronomes* was still claiming, as late as 1962, that the leaves 'are treated like spinach. The taste does not please everybody; but there is at least agreement on finding it refreshing.' 'Agreement among survivors, one supposes,' Root laconically comments. Professor Foust has located a discussion of rhubarb from the superintendent of exotics at the gardens of Versailles in a letter to the English botanist Anthony Fothergill in 1785. They had made successfully a marmalade of the stalks, which they found acted as a mild laxative: this anticipates the principal use of rhubarb stalks in French cookery, as a compôte or candied sweetmeat, their purpose largely medicinal. 'The superintendent also reported,' Foust goes on, 'the use of leaves in soups "to which they impart an agreeable acidity, like that of sorrel".'

******

If we have now progressed as far as a decent plant, a recipe or two and a general idea that rhubarb would make a satisfactory spring fruit (even if, pedantically, it was thought a vegetable) we still have to see supplies in the markets. This omission was rectified by an enterprising south-London gardener called Joseph Myatt in 1808 or 1809. His achievement was later recorded by the indefatigable Henry Mayhew (1861, vol. 1, p. 84):

> I may instance the introduction of rhubarb, which was comparatively unknown until Mr. Myatt, now of Deptford, cultivated it thirty years ago. He then, for the first time, carried seven bundles of rhubarb into the Borough market. Of these he could only sell three, and he took four back with him. Mr. Myatt could not recollect the price he received for the first rhubarb he ever sold in public, but he told me that the stalks were only about half the substance of those he now produces. People laughed at him for offering "physic pies," but he persevered.

This little paragraph underlines the significant role played by a single grower; it also stresses how rapid improvements of breeding and selection were undertaken by Myatt and his competitors in the first years of commercial exploitation of the plant. An infinite number of new varieties were developed – so infinite, indeed, that the Royal Horticultural Society had to intervene in 1884 to bring taxonomic order to the nurserymen's chaos. By mid-century, Mayhew estimated that 7,200 dozen bunches of rhubarb were sold at Covent Garden, 48,000 at Borough market in Southwark, 28,800 at Spitalfields, 2,400 at Farringdon close to the City, and 4,800 dozen at Portman market in the West End. This would seem to confirm Mayhew's own assessment that rhubarb was more food for the common man than something to adorn dainty tables in Mayfair. Another Victorian journalist, George Dodd (1856), reported that 2,100 tons of rhubarb were sold in London markets in 1850, of which only 150 tons were purveyed through Covent Garden.

Myatt was renowned both for his rhubarb and his strawberries. The two fruits go well together, as you can see from the recipes. By coincidence, another Victorian family of nurserymen, the Osbaldestons of Baguley in Cheshire, specialized in the same pair. John Osbaldeston was the first to supply rhubarb to Manchester, in 1833. He maintained a virtual monopoly for many years. Fifty years on, the firm was to pioneer the commercial growing of strawberries in the region (Scola 1992).

Mayhew sensed that rhubarb was part of a broader process of change in the diet of the Victorian urban consumer. He made a perceptive comment (1861, vol. 1, p. 159):

> A gentleman … considers that the great change [in street trading in the previous fifty years] is not so much in what has ceased to be sold, but in the introduction of fresh articles into street-traffic – such as pine-apples and Brazil-nuts, rhubarb and cucumbers, ham-sandwiches, ginger-beer, &c.

One reason for nurserymen to experiment with new varieties was to improve sweetness and delicacy of flavour: to distance rhubarb from 'physic pie'. The single most important discovery, quite early in the century, was finding that rhubarb could be forced, accelerating its arrival in the shops, and reducing its astringency. As with so much about this plant, it was by way of an accident. A bed of rhubarb in the Chelsea Physic Garden was buried beneath spoil thrown up by workmen digging a trench in 1815. When they came to remove the debris, it was found the stalks were blanched, sweeter and more tender. It took little time for more organized trials to be undertaken and there were many contributions to the trade literature of the time on the best method of forcing. In the main, the preferred systems involved large boxes or frames piled with compost and manure to promote heat, or large pots put in the vine house or some such shelter, or boxes placed in the mushroom cellar. These were all more or less elaborate schemes that differ only from open-ground forcing under inverted pots or dustbins which we are familiar with in our own back gardens in that a certain amount of heat was involved. If you want to get proper early crops, you have to have the roots at 55 to 65 degrees Fahrenheit.

The big innovation in forcing occurred in West Yorkshire, in an area now called 'The Rhubarb Triangle' (more exactly a square) between the towns of Leeds, Wakefield, Bradford and Rothwell. Rhubarb was marketed outside London. I have already mentioned the Osbaldeston family in Manchester; there were large supplies available in Edinburgh; Birmingham had growers sending into the markets from at least the 1820s; and the earliest grower in Leeds was one Appleby of Hunslet in 1819. In the late 1870s, however, Joseph Whitwell of Kirkstall (a Leeds suburb) took the forcing business one step further by constructing sheds devoted only to growing rhubarb. Yorkshire was an ideal situation. The soil was good; there were plentiful and cheap supplies of coal to heat the forcing sheds; there was lots of manure and composting material available from the horse-drawn traffic of the town, the sewage works and slaughterhouses, and particularly the woollen mills for shoddy and other by-products all of which contributed nitrogen. And the climate was perfect for rhubarb. A touch of frost in the autumn would get the roots into top condition for bringing on in the sheds.

This happy combination of agricultural circumstance gave rise to much activity. The Yorkshire season was early: sticks could be in the market before Christmas. The district was soon the preferred London supplier and many farmers in the Triangle built sheds and turned their land over to it. Every week-night during the three-month season, a train left Ardsley station laden with up to 200 tons of produce. The last Rhubarb Express left in 1966. There used once to be up to 200 growers but there are now 'around ten', and there were still more than a thousand acres given over to the crop in 1966 (it is now down to less than 400).

Roots that are to be forced are usually two or three years old. They will not have been previously cropped. They do best if they are exposed to some hard frosts before being brought indoors for forcing. The roots are then only harvested for one year. A well-grown root of the Victoria variety might weigh between 28 and 56 lb. (And a recycled orange box of sticks ready for the market weighed 84 lb until the Leeds and District Market Gardeners Association redesigned the boxes to weigh only 14 lb.) Oldroyd's, one of the champions and stalwarts of the trade in Yorkshire, also remark on their website that they only crop their outdoor roots for three years before replacement.

The rhubarb trade over the last century or more has depended on the improved varieties that were developed from the 1850s, although plant breeding and selection has carried on, most notably at the Stockbridge horticultural research and development station at Cawood, near Selby. Their modern varieties, Stockbridge Cropper, Stockbridge Arrow, Stockbridge Guardsman and Cawood Delight are well regarded. Two of the oldest varieties, Prince Albert and Victoria, are those selected by Joseph Myatt himself, while a gardening neighbour in south London is credited with Hawkes' Champagne. Ben Asquith of Brandy Carr Nurseries, whose website is informative, says that his forebears (who began forcing rhubarb during the First World War) relied on Prince Albert, Victoria, Fenton's Special – a variety named for the Fenton family who grew rhubarb at Tingley in Morley in the 1930s – and Grey Giant. An important modern variety is Timperley Early.

Although rhubarb has come once more into favour, as chefs and cookery writers seek unfamiliar flavours and combinations to tickle our palates, there was a pronounced decline in its popularity in the middle years of the twentieth century. The reasons advanced are various. Yorkshire growers tell of the decimation of their resources during the Second World War by a Ministry of Food eager to utilize every spare ingredient. In the first instance, fuel and fertilising materials were harder to come by in the war years; in the second, Ministry officials noticed that the growers left young roots to flourish unharvested. This was essential to their successful forcing in their third year of life. However, the Ministry insisted that they be cropped and the sticks pulped for jam. This meant there were no roots in proper condition for forcing. If this were not enough, the tremendous accession of new fruits and sub-tropical produce in British markets in the '50s and '60s meant that rhubarb had serious, and sweet, competition. We lost our taste for it.

Without doubt, the British adopted rhubarb with greater enthusiasm, and earlier, than most other countries. But the recipes I have collected here make plain that its cookery was not confined to Britain alone. First there was the Empire, old and new. Plants and seed went to America and later in the nineteenth century much work was done by plant breeders such as Luther Burbank to develop new varieties. Burbank took advantage of the fact that rhubarb had followed the English settlers to Australia and New Zealand in the southern hemisphere. Their plants were acclimatized to the seasons in reverse and he capitalized on this to breed winter-cropping varieties for America which reached the market much earlier than competitors. California became an important centre for early rhubarb production although today most is grown in the northern states of Washington, Oregon and Michigan.

In Europe, too, rhubarb was embraced as a new ingredient, especially in northern countries. In France, Spain and Italy, its appearance usually had medicinal undertones, although in the 1960s and 1970s it began to be adopted by *nouvelle cuisine* chefs such as Alain Chapel and the Troisgros brothers, each of whom included recipes for tarts in their ground-breaking books. More recently, the chefs who have led the latest changes in restaurant cooking, such as Ferran Adrià in Spain (and Heston Blumenthal in England), have not been shy of experimenting. In the Low Countries, Germany and Scandinavia – as well as in parts of eastern Europe – rhubarb was widely adopted in the nineteenth century and recipes that have met with success in these countries are included in the anthology which follows.

A NOTE ON THE RECIPES

Unless otherwise stated, the recipes are sufficient for four people. In most instances, I have given metric and imperial measures but there are a few where the quantities remain in cups and spoons. In general, when pepper is mentioned, I mean black pepper, freshly ground.

CHAPTER ONE

RHUBARB AND MEAT
A DISH FIT FOR A KING

They sent us also some stalks and suckers of rhubarb, preserved in the gravy of lamb. They are very refreshing and laxative, of a delicate taste, and very much esteemed at this time of year... They are cultivated for the King's table, in the neighbourhood of Laer where the governor is obliged annually to make him a present of the same.

Cornelis le Bruin 1737 (1711), vol. 2, pp. 188–9

This account of rhubarb in Persian cookery is from a famous Dutch traveller to the Levant and the Middle East. It underlines the fact that the plant was eaten in those parts far earlier than ever it was in Europe. Note, however, that its use still had medicinal undertones. If recourse is had to medieval cookery texts from the Arab world, rhubarb is plainly in evidence in the first and most famous of these, the Baghdad Cookery Book (*Kitāb al-Tabīkh*) of the thirteenth century. The name of the dish is *Rībāsiyya*, and *rībās* is rhubarb. A later version of the recipe, from *The Description of Familiar Foods* (Rodinson, Arberry and Perry 2001, p. 312), reads as follows:

RĪBĀSIYYA
It is boiled meat stewed with spices on which you throw a bit of onion cut up small. Then squeeze the juice of rhubarb and throw it on it. Then add some peeled sweet almonds, pounded and made into a paste, and crumble a bunch of dry mint on top of it, and leave it on the fire awhile until it settles, and take it up, so understand that.

This dish in Iran, its place of origin, now goes under the name of *khoresht-e-rivas* (literally rhubarb sauce, although we would think of it rather as a stew). Persians prefer to have it with a lot of liquid and a lot of rice, whilst in the West it is offered with more meat, less liquid and rice. There are countless versions, most often with lamb, although Sally Butcher's, from her book *Persia in Peckham*, is with chicken. She comments that it is her mother's favourite Persian recipe. There is a very good recipe for lamb and rhubarb *khoresh(t)* in Jane Grigson's *Fruit Book*, and another, with beef this time, in Claudia Roden's book of Middle Eastern food.

Often the *khoresht* is spiced, as well as benefiting from mint as in the medieval recipe. Jane Grigson suggests saffron, Claudia Roden cinnamon or allspice, another version lists cloves and cinnamon.

The sharpness of rhubarb in these recipes is offset by butter or oil, but my introduction to the combination of rhubarb and meat was unfortunate. I was slimming at the time, and I cut the amount of butter in a *khoresh* recipe drastically. It left me gasping. There was something elemental about it. I could imagine the ancient tribes of Siberia eating a prehistoric version of the recipe: rancid butter, rhubarb and deep-frozen dinosaur. I reached for the nearest sweetener that came to hand – a jar of quince jam. It was fine. Better I think than mango chutney. But the real lesson is don't cut the butter.

Khoresht-e-Rivas

1 skinned chicken
a little butter
1 large onion, chopped
1 teaspoon ground turmeric
½ bottle sour grape juice (or 2 tablespoons lemon juice)
2 dessertspoons fresh or pickled sour grapes (optional)
salt and pepper

1 small bunch mint (or 60 g dried mint)
1 small bunch parsley (or 60 g dried)
1 small bunch coriander (or 60 g dried)
1 large bundle rhubarb, washed and peeled (if large, mature
  stalks)

Chop your chicken: separate legs from thighs, and halve the breasts, leaving it all on the bone. Melt the butter in a pan, and toss in the onion and turmeric. Once the onion has started to soften, add in the chicken and seal all over. Add the sour grape juice, sour grapes, salt and pepper, and enough water to cover, bring to the boil and set to simmer. As an alternative to the above, you can just place the chicken, onion, turmeric and seasoning in the pan with the verjuice and water and bring to the boil – but I believe that frying best releases the flavour of the turmeric.

In the meantime sort, wash, drain and chop your herbs (if using dried herbs you will have needed to soak them first). Pour a little oil in a frying-pan, and fry the herbs, stirring constantly so that they do not catch. Cook for around 8 minutes and then add to the casserole. Continue to cook for around half an hour until the chicken is cooked through.

Chop the rhubarb into pieces approximately 3cm long and lower it into the sauce. Cook the whole thing for around another 10 minutes, check the seasoning, and ladle carefully into a serving dish.

Serve with plain basmati rice, yoghurt and fresh raw garlic.

Sally Butcher 2007, p. 150

The next recipe was given me by Ingirid Eunson of Nesbister on Shetland. It is an adaptation from Claudia Roden. Ingirid urges us to use Shetland lamb if possible. The sheep are tiny and hardy, and they graze on hillsides rich with heather and thyme. She remarks, 'This is a popular dish in the household even with fussy visitors.' While she suggests serving it with plain rice or mashed potatoes, the Persian way might be to cook the rice with some butter left in the bottom of the pan so that the grains form a light brown crust.

SHETLAND LAMB KHORESH

oil or butter
1 large onion, sliced
1 shoulder of Shetland lamb, weighing between 500 g and 1 kg
  / 1–2 lb, boned and cubed
salt, pepper
¾ tsp allspice
225–450 g / ½–1 lb of rhubarb
juice of half a lemon

Heat 2–3 tablespoons of oil or 2 of butter in a large saucepan and fry the onion until soft and golden. Add the meat and brown it. Cover with water, season with salt, pepper and allspice. Simmer for about ¾ hour or until tender.

Trim rhubarb and cut into 2-inch lengths. Add to the meat and simmer for a further 10–15 minutes. Stir in the lemon juice.

QORMA-E-RAHWASH

Afghanistan, Iran's neighbour to the east, boasts a cookery that blends influences from Persia, the wider Islamic world, the Indian sub-continent, as well as the plains and deserts of central Asia. Qorma is their word for stew, their equivalent of khoresh. This recipe comes from Helen Saberi's *Noshe Djan, Afghan Food and Cookery*. She notes that in the traditional classification of foods, rhubarb was considered 'cold', in other words a counterbalance to 'hot' spices and meat, as well as performing the cleansing and purifying functions that are accorded it in the West.

3 onions, finely chopped
75 ml / 5 tbsp vegetable oil
700 g / 1½ lb boneless lamb, cubed
1 tbsp tomato purée
1 tsp ground coriander
salt and pepper
450 g / 1 lb rhubarb
small bunch fresh coriander or mint, finely chopped

Fry the onions in the vegetable oil over a medium heat until soft and golden brown. Add the meat and continue frying until brown. Stir in the tomato purée and fry for a minute or two. Add about half a cupful of water, the ground coriander and salt and pepper and bring to the boil. Turn down the heat and simmer until the meat is cooked.

Meanwhile wash the rhubarb and cut into 5 cm / 2 inch lengths. Boil in a small amount of water until it is soft, but not disintegrating.

Just before serving, drain the rhubarb and place over the top of the *qorma*. Garnish with coriander or mint. Serve with rice.

Serving rhubarb with meat was uncommon in Victorian Britain but has become more widely practised today. Recipes for pork and chicken follow below, but it is always possible to take the rhubarb sauce recipe in the chapter on fish and use it as a condiment or accompaniment to many richer and fatter meats: venison is one, some even advocate it with roast beef. Birds benefit from it: rhubarb goes well with squab pigeon, and excellently with duck.

COUNTRY THATCHED PIE

225 g / 8 oz rhubarb
1 tbsp sugar
225 g / 8 oz pickling onions
225 g / 8 oz button mushrooms
225 g / 8 oz carrots
1 tbsp / 15 ml oil
450 g / 1 lb pork fillet
1 tbsp wholemeal flour
salt and ground black pepper
400 ml / ¾ pt beef stock
2 tbsp freshly chopped parsley
frozen puff pastry to cover the pie dish

Slice into one-inch pieces the washed and trimmed rhubarb. Put in a bowl and sprinkle with sugar. Cover and stand some hours or overnight, then drain. Leave the mushrooms and onions whole, but wipe the mushrooms and peel the onions. Scrub the carrots and cut into large sticks. Fry the vegetables in a heavy-based pan until tender. Dice the pork. Shake the flour over the pile of meat to coat it evenly. Fry the pork and the vegetables together for 5 minutes to brown and seal the meat. Add the rhubarb and the stock and season to taste. Bring to the boil, cover and simmer 25–30 minutes or until tender. Strew with parsley, and turn the cooked mixture into a 2½-pint pie dish. Sprinkle it with more parsley and cool. Heat the oven to 200°C/400°F. Roll out the pastry and cover the pie. Decorate the pie with the trimmings and crimp the edges with the back of a fork. Secure the trimmings with water, then glaze the pie with beaten egg. Make two vents in the crust to allow steam to escape. Bake for about 25 minutes or thereabouts, or until it is golden brown, and the pastry puffed up.

Christine France 1985

Loin of Pork with Rhubarb

It is possible to cook pork chops straightforwardly in your normal fashion and accompany them with a simple rhubarb sauce such as that proposed for mackerel on page 48. Ham, boiled, baked or fried as gammon, is pleasant with rhubarb too – rather on the principle of ham and pineapple or apricot. Otherwise, here is a recipe outlined by the chef Joyce Molyneux from her former restaurant in Dartmouth, The Carved Angel, and contained in her *Carved Angel Cookery Book*.

1 kg / 2 lb loin of pork, skinned and chined
orange peel (no pith), blanched and sliced in strips
parsley, chopped
salt and pepper
250 ml / 8 fl oz white wine
250 ml / 8 fl oz stock
110 g / 4 oz granulated sugar
220 g / 8 oz rhubarb

Lard the joint of meat with the orange peel and parsley, stuffing them into slits between meat and bone and under the fat. Season with salt and pepper and leave the joint in a roasting pan with the white wine for up to 4 hours, basting at intervals. Add the stock and roast, fat side downwards, in an oven preheated to 190°C/375°F/gas mark 5 for 30 minutes. Turn the joint over and continue for another 30 minutes.

Meanwhile, make a syrup with the sugar and 300 ml / 10 fl oz cold water. Bring to the boil until the sugar is dissolved, then simmer for 5 minutes. Cut the rhubarb into short lengths and poach in the syrup for 5 minutes until tender. Lift out with a slotted spoon.

Make a gravy of the pan juices, skimming off any fat. Place the joint in a serving dish with the rhubarb disposed around it.

FILLET OF PORK WITH A RHUBARB STUFFING

Here the pork fillets are flattened out and rolled around a stuffing, rather like beef olives. There is a recipe like this in Pamela Westland's *Taste of the Country* although others have suggested more elaborate sauces to finish the dish.

2 fillets of pork (each approximately 350 g / 12 oz)
3 sticks prepared rhubarb, finely chopped
100 g / 4 oz fresh white breadcrumbs
1 large onion, chopped
1 tbsp parsley, chopped
300 ml / ½ pint dry cider
75 g / 3 oz butter
1 teaspoon of sugar
salt and pepper
1 tbsp fresh ginger, grated

Cut each fillet of pork in half lengthwise, but do not cut right through. Open the fillets out and beat them flat with a mallet. Chop one stick of rhubarb and mix with the breadcrumbs, half the chopped onion and the parsley. Moisten with some of the cider. Spread the pork with the rhubarb mixture and roll into two rolls secured with string or cocktail sticks. Seal these all round in 2 oz butter in a casserole. Pour the rest of the cider over it, and add the sugar, salt and pepper. Cover and cook at 220°C/425°F/gas mark 7 for 30 minutes. Take out the rolls and keep them warm. Drain the meat dish of fat and reserve the gravy. Melt the rest of the butter and fry the remainder of the rhubarb and onion. Add the grated ginger. Add back the juices from the cooking pan and reduce by boiling until they are sufficiently tasty.

CHICKEN AND RHUBARB

Chicken, too, can be enhanced by a rhubarb sauce and it can be given added zest with ginger, lemon or lime juice, spices like cinnamon and nutmeg or herbs like fresh green coriander.

8 chicken drumsticks
salt and pepper
50 g / 2 oz butter
½ small onion, chopped
1 tbsp flour
14 g / ½ oz brown sugar
2 tsp fresh ginger, grated
150 ml / 5 fl oz water
juice of 1 lemon or lime
3 sticks rhubarb, sliced in short lengths

Season the drumsticks well, and fry them in butter on all sides together with the onion. Remove the drumsticks. Stir flour, sugar and ginger into the onion and butter in the pan. Stir them and scrape them together for 2 minutes. Add the water and lemon or lime juice and cook, stirring until it is smooth. More liquid and seasoning may be added if necessary. Put the chicken joints back in the pan and add the rhubarb. Cover and cook very gently for about 45 minutes. Serve with rice.

ROAST PUFFIN AND RHUBARB JAM

Puffin is popular on Iceland and The Faeroes. The Icelanders smoke them and sell the ready-prepared breasts, described as gamey, 'with a marine twang'. They also cook them in milk. The anthropologist Anthony Jackson reported on a Faeroese recipe in Jessica Kuper's *Anthropologist's Cookbook*: 'First pluck and draw the birds, then singe and truss them. Place bacon on their breasts, and roast at 205°C/400°F for 15–20 minutes. Remove the bacon to allow the breasts to brown before they are completely cooked, and serve with brown gravy, boiled potatoes and rhubarb jam.'

An Icelandic recipe might entail plucking and drawing the birds, then washing the meat in salted water. Sometimes the breasts alone are marinaded, for instance with rosemary, schnapps and oil, then quickly fried. Other recipes suggest barding (i.e. laying fat bacon over) the meat with bacon and cooking it slowly in a mixture of milk and water. A sauce can be made from the cooking liquid, sweetened and flavoured with some sort of jam or jelly, maybe redcurrant or, indeed, rhubarb.

Eating puffins in the Faeroes is not surprising, the food supply is somewhat limited. They are however regarded as suitable for important occasions. They were served at a conference in the Faeroes attended by the Shetland archivist. It is said he walked out in disgust. Shetlanders have a soft spot for puffins, and the no-smoking sign can be seen with the cancellation sign crossing an image of the bird. No words are needed.

CHAPTER TWO

RHUBARB AND FISH

We have already noted Kitchiner's suggestion that mackerel be served with rhubarb sauce rather than the customary gooseberries. Mistress Margaret Dods commented in her recipe for mackerel that normally they are served with a fennel sauce or a mixture of fennel and parsley with melted butter. 'The French', she said, 'cook mackerel with fine herbs, champagne and butter. Nor in London are the days quite gone by –

'When Mackerel seemed delightful to their eyes,
Though dressed with incoherent gooseberries.'

The writer Theodora FitzGibbon suggested that the combination of mackerel and rhubarb was a speciality of Bristol and the west country. Certainly, the next recipe, including as it does the west-country beverage of choice, cider, was given me by Margaret Brown, of the Simonsbath Hotel on Exmoor, who found it in an old Penzance cookbook.

BAKED MACKEREL WITH A SPICED RHUBARB SAUCE

8 cleaned, filleted mackerel
8 bay leaves
24 black peppercorns
salt and pepper
6 tbsp dry cider
small amount of butter

for the sauce
450 g / 1 lb chopped
   rhubarb
8 tbsp dry cider
a squeeze of lemon
½ tsp each of salt, mace,
   nutmeg, cinnamon
4 tbsp soft brown sugar

Lay the fillets flat in a buttered dish. Place a bay leaf, peppercorns, butter and salt on each. Roll them up and pour cider over each of them; dot with butter. Cover and bake at 180°C/350°F/gas mark 4 about 40 minutes. Meanwhile, the ingredients for the sauce should be cooked over a low flame until soft and purée-like. It can be sieved if liked. Add a little more cider if too dry. To serve, pour the sauce down the centre of the mackerel fillets, and sprinkle with chopped parsley.

Whether it was indeed the invention of Cornishmen, Bristolians or someone else, the Irish also claim mackerel and rhubarb for their own. Alan Davidson recommended a recipe from the Irish Sea Fisheries Board in his handbook *North Atlantic Seafood* which also rolls and stuffs the fillets and bakes them in the oven.

MACKEREL WITH RHUBARB

60 g / 2 oz margarine or butter
1 large onion, finely chopped
250 g / 8 oz rhubarb, chopped
salt and pepper
2 tbsp toasted breadcrumbs
1 kg / 2 lb mackerel fillets

for the sauce
450 g / 1 lb rhubarb
2 tbsp sugar
2 tbsp water
a little grated lemon rind

Melt the margarine or butter and sweat the chopped onion. When it is transparent, add the chopped rhubarb, pepper and salt. Cook gently for 5 minutes. Stir in the breadcrumbs. Lay the fillets flat, skin side down, and spread the stuffing on them. Roll them up, and place in a greased dish in a preheated oven at 200°C/400°F/gas mark 6 for 15–20 minutes.

While cooking, put the ingredients for the sauce in a pan to stew until the rhubarb is soft. This will take 10 minutes or a little longer. Put the sauce through the blender, or sieve it. Serve it hot or cold. Alan Davidson suggested that some people might like more sugar than the recipe proposes.

PLAICE WITH ORANGE AND RHUBARB SAUCE

8 plaice fillets
25 g / 1 oz butter

for the sauce
225 g / 8 oz rhubarb
juice of 3 oranges
2 tsp coarse-cut marmalade
salt and pepper
¼ tsp cayenne pepper

Set the oven at 180°C/350°F/gas mark 4. Skin the plaice fillets and roll them up, skin side innermost. Grease a shallow oven-proof dish with half the butter. Put the fish in the dish and dot with the rest of the butter, then cover with foil and bake for 20 minutes or until tender.

For the sauce, trim the washed rhubarb, and cut into half-inch slices. Put the orange juice in a small pan with the rhubarb, marmalade, salt, pepper and cayenne. Bring to the boil slowly, and cook gently for 5 minutes, so that the rhubarb is tender and the liquid reduced to a syrup. Pour it over the plaice and serve hot.

Christine France 1985

· BACON AND SCALLOP KEBABS

The American nutritionist and home economist Evelyn DeNike wrote a book of rhubarb recipes in 1964 which caught early the possibility of pairing rhubarb with a number of savoury flavours. She suggested scallops, as here described, but others have proposed a rhubarb sauce with pan-fried foie gras. In both cases, the smooth and rich texture of the main ingredient is pleasingly lightened by the acidity of the sauce or accompaniment.

The idea is that the kebabs consist of skewers threaded with scallops, pieces of green pepper and short lengths of rhubarb wrapped in rashers of streaky bacon. The kebabs should be grilled until the bacon is crisp. As you turn the skewers, baste them with a mixture of fresh orange juice and olive oil.

An alternative way of proceeding might be to pan-fry the scallops in butter and accompany them with a rhubarb sauce made as below, or perhaps one flavoured with thyme rather than orange and ginger. I have also seen a sauce made with fresh ginger, lemon grass and kaffir lime leaves.

RHUBARB SAUCE

From my comments so far, it will be clear that there are many possibilities for rhubarb sauce. As regards fish, for instance, people now advocate it being served with fried fillets of John Dory, or with salmon steaks, as well as the usual suspects.

228 g / 8 oz rhubarb, cut in 1-inch slices
1 shallot or small red onion, chopped
juice and grated zest of an orange
4 tbsp of water
1 tsp fresh ginger, grated
salt and pepper

Put everything together in a pan and cover it. Cook it on a low heat for 10 minutes. Put it through a blender, and adjust the seasoning.

CHAPTER THREE

RHUBARB AS A VEGETABLE

On the last birthday which George the Fourth lived to see, the flagstaff at Lerwick Castle (i.e. Fort Charlotte) fell prostrate to the earth, which was after considered a prophetic omen. The very same pole is now so insufficiently propped up that all well-wishers of her present Majesty should subscribe to raise one... Loyal as the inhabitants of Shetland are, however, their woods and forests could scarcely supply so much as a pair of Dutch clogs... The tallest and grandest tree I saw during my stay on the island was a stalk of rhubarb near seven feet tall, which had run to seed, and waved its head majestically in a garden below the fort, looking quite shady and ornamental. It had been planted by some officers, and really did them great credit.

Catherine Sinclair 1840, p. 130

EASTERMAN GIANTS

There is something a little comic about the search for the true rhubarb. While it absorbed the energies of botanists and explorers all over the Continent, there were many home-grown medicinal plants offering purges to generations of country folk without the bother of crossing Tartary. One of these magical herbs was bistort (*Polygonum bistorta*), which has retained the affection of many in the Lake District and northern counties. Geoffrey Grigson, in his *Englishman's Flora*, suggests the real reason for eating the leaves of this plant was to promote conception, but in general it seems to have been consumed as a springtime purge.

Bistort went under a variety of names: Easter Giant, Easter Ledges, Easter Ledger and Easter Mangiants (deriving from the French *manger*, but if differently spelled becoming Easterman Giants!) were the names in the north; but it was also known as Patience Dock and Passion Dock and Gentle Dock as well as Snakeweed (for its quality as an antidote to snake bite).

Geoffrey Grigson quotes a recipe for Easter Ledge pudding:

Pick young Easter Ledge leaves, and drop them with leaves of Dandelion, Lady's Mantle, or Nettle into boiling water and cook for 20 minutes. Strain and chop. Add a little boiled barley, a chopped egg (hard-boiled), butter, pepper, salt. Heat in a saucepan and press into a pudding basin. Serve with veal or bacon.

A recipe for Easterman Giants was obtained from the Raughton-head Women's Institute near Carlisle by Richard Mabey when compiling his *Flora Britannica*. It proposed:

A small quantity of nettles, cabbage or young leaves and shoots of Brussels sprouts, kale or curly greens; 3 or 4 dandelion or dock leaves; a good handful of Easterman Giants; 2 or 3 gooseberry or blackcurrant leaves; and some cooked barley. Put the greens in the water and cook them. Chop and mix with the barley. Serve with or without eggs, or beat the eggs in.

These recipes are very close to the instructions revealed by an interview of an elderly resident of Millom in Cumbria by members of the Millom and District Oral History Group. She called it simply 'herb pudding', but it contained Easterman Giants, nettles, dandelions, blackcurrant leaves, hawthorn leaves and sour dockings. These were chopped up with some spring cabbage and a few sticks of rhubarb, mixed with barley and a couple of beaten eggs, then boiled as a pudding and served with lamb and mint sauce. 'It will give you diarrhoea like fun,' she said, 'but it would clean your blood.'

Sabzi Rahwash, Spinach with Rhubarb and Dill

In the same way as their Persian neighbours, the Afghans use rhubarb in savoury dishes. This recipe comes from Helen Saberi's description of their cookery in *Noshe Djan, Afghan Food and Cookery*. She notes it can be served with a *pilau* or a *qorma* or meat stew. The leeks in the recipe should in reality be an Afghan vegetable, *gandana*, which is akin to Chinese chives. Some European cooks replace them with spring onions, but Helen advises leeks.

99 g / 2 lb spinach
450 g / 1 lb leeks, cleaned and chopped
75 ml / 5 tbsp vegetable oil
2 tbsp powdered dill weed
salt and pepper
50 g / 2 oz rhubarb

Wash the spinach thoroughly, remove the stems and chop roughly. Wash the leeks well and chop into small pieces.

Heat 50 ml / 2 tbsp of vegetable oil in a pan and fry the leeks over a medium to high heat. When they are soft but not brown, add the spinach and stir continuously until the spinach reduces. Reduce the heat, cover, and continue to cook gently, stirring occasionally, until the oil comes to the surface. Then add the dill, salt and pepper. Add a little water if necessary.

While the spinach is cooking, skin and wash the rhubarb and cut it into 2.5 cm / 1 in. lengths. Fry it briefly in the remaining 25 ml / 2 tbsp of oil over a medium heat, without letting it brown, then add it to the spinach and cook for a further half an hour or until it is sufficiently cooked.

RHUBARB AND POTATOES

This Polish recipe combines rhubarb and new potatoes. It comes from the classic domestic handbook by Maria Ochorowicz-Monatowa, *Universalna ksiazka kucharska*, first published in 1910.

5 stalks of rhubarb	Broth
450 g / 1 lb of new potatoes	*2 cups of water*
1 tbsp butter	*6 dried mushrooms*
1 tbsp flour	*1 onion, sliced*
1 heaped tsp chives, chopped	*1 bay leaf*
1 clove of garlic, crushed	*a few sprigs of dill*
salt and pepper	*salt and pepper*

Let the broth simmer about half an hour to extract the flavour from the mushrooms.

Wash and clean the rhubarb and cut it into 2.5 cm /1 inch slices and put it in the broth. When it is tender, drain and reserve the liquid. Meanwhile, boil the potatoes separately.

In a third saucepan, make a roux by browning the butter, then adding the flour and cooking it well. Add a cup of the broth and stir until it is smooth. If it is too thick add more broth. Add chives and crushed garlic. Season to taste. Add the rhubarb and potatoes to the sauce and cook gently until thoroughly heated.

FRUIT MOOS

This recipe is inspired by the Mennonite *More-with-Less Cookbook* by Doris Longacre, published in 1976. The author was anxious to show there was more to food than high-protein, meat-based dishes and drew largely on German, Polish and Russian traditions. The *Moos* (a German word) was akin to northern European fruit soups and was usually made with dried fruits, or tart fruits like gooseberries, plums or cherries. It could be served alongside a meat course of ham and fried potatoes or as a sweet dish to finish the meal. It was popular for Sundays as it could be made the day before, avoiding the need to cook on the Sabbath. Mennonites are strict Protestant Anabaptists named for their teacher Menno Simons (*d.* 1561). The Amish are Mennonite at root. The first Mennonites were in Switzerland and Germany but spread eastwards, due to persecution, and later came to America, where they flourish today.

1 quart of rhubarb, prepared and cut into short lengths
700 ml / 1 ½ pints milk or water
100 g / 4 oz honey or castor sugar
4 tbsp cornflour
300 ml / 10 fl oz double cream

Heat in a heavy pan the fruit, water or milk and honey or sugar. Simmer gently until the fruit is tender.

Slake the cornflour with some cold milk in a small bowl. Add the cream and mix to a paste. Pour this into the simmering fruit and cook over a low heat until it thickens. Should it need extra sweetness, you can add more honey or sugar. It can be served hot or cold.

Rhubarb Mint Salad

I first came across this pleasing combination in Nathalie Hambro's imaginative book *Particular Delights* (1981). It can be made more of a composition by mixing rhubarb with cucumber and adding some leaves of rocket along with the mint. Other people suggest a salad of rhubarb, mint and melon as being refreshing, aromatic and all that a salad should be. Another combination of rhubarb and mint can be seen in the rhubarb jelly recipe at the end of the chapter on jams.

500 g / 1 lb forced rhubarb stems
1 tsp brown sugar
1 tbsp red wine vinegar
5 tbsp extra virgin olive oil
salt and pepper
10 mint leaves

Slice the rhubarb finely and put it in a serving dish. Strew it with brown sugar. Marinate for an hour. Make the dressing and pour it over the sugar and rhubarb. Shred the mint and scatter over the salad immediately before serving.

RHUBARB AND LENTIL DIP

This is a recipe with a delicate flavour and it is best to add the ingredients cautiously to get the right balance.

75 g / 3 oz brown lentils
1 small carrot, cleaned and roughly sliced
1 small onion, peeled and sliced
cottage cheese
lemon juice
1 or 2 sticks of rhubarb, chopped
salt, pepper and granulated sugar
1 tsp mint, chopped

Pour near-boiling water over the lentils and let them soak for at least half an hour. Cook them gently with the carrot and onion until tender.

Strain off the excess water and add an equal quantity of cottage cheese, or slightly less, and a squeeze of lemon juice. Add 1 or 2 sticks of finely chopped rhubarb and liquidize. Season with salt, sugar, and freshly ground black pepper. Top with chopped mint. Serve with crisps or sticks of cucumber or celery.

CHAPTER FOUR

RHUBARB SOUPS

The Mock Turtle sighed deeply, and began, to sing, in a
voice sometimes choked with sobs, to sing this:
    'Beautiful Soup, so rich and green,
    Waiting in a hot tureen!
    Who for such dainties would not stoop?
    Soup of the evening, beautiful soup!
    Soup of the evening, beautiful soup!
    Beau–ootiful Soo–oop!
    Beau–ootiful Soo–oop!
    Soo–oop of the e–e–evening,
    Beautiful beautiful soup!'
             Lewis Carroll, *Alice's Adventures in Wonderland*

STEPHANA MALCOLM'S SPRING FRUIT SOUP

The manuscript recipe book of Stephana Malcolm preserved
in the National Library of Scotland and discussed in Olive M.
Geddes' revealing *The Laird's Kitchen* is a positive treasure-
trove of early rhubarb recipes, including this, the first rhubarb
soup I know of. Her mother had started the family tradition of
compiling recipe books and this recipe comes from a collection
dating from 1790 or 1791. It is possible Stephana got the recipe
from the wife of one of her brothers for, like many other Scots,
three of them served abroad. One was Governor of Bombay,
another became an admiral during the Napoleonic Wars, and
the third a vice-admiral. Perhaps the recipe had an eastern
origin:

> clean as above 4 dozen sticks of Rhubarb, blanch it in
> water 3 or 4 minutes drain it on a sieve & put it in a stew-
> pan with 2 Onions sliced, a Carrot, an oz of lean ham &
> a good bit of butter let it stew gently over a slow fire till

tender then put in 2 quarts of good consommé to which
add 2 or 3 ounces of breadcrumbs, boil 15 minutes skim
off all the fat season with salt & Cayenne Pepper pass it
through a tammis & serve up with fried bread.

Geddes 1994

Clearly the amount of rhubarb in this recipe is out of all
proportion to the other ingredients, and one finds the amount
reduced in Jane Grigson's adaptation of the recipe in her *Fruit
Book*. For instance, she replaces Stephana's 4 dozen sticks of
rhubarb with 1 lb only.

SPRING SOUP

500 g / 1 lb rhubarb
2 onions, sliced
1 carrot, chopped
30 g / 1 oz uncooked ham or gammon, chopped
60 g / 2 oz butter
2.25 litres / 4 pints chicken stock
90 g / 3 oz fresh white breadcrumbs
salt, cayenne pepper, sugar
little bread cubes fried in butter

Peel the rhubarb. Slice the stems longitudinally and then
into small pieces. Blanch for 3 or 4 minutes. Drain it
and put it in a large pan with the onion, carrot, ham
and butter. Stew gently until the rhubarb is tender.
Add the stock, breadcrumbs and seasoning, then heat
it thoroughly. Liquidize or sieve. Serve the croûtons
separately.

MEG DODS' SPRING FRUIT SOUP

As if to emphasize the importance of Edinburgh in the early cultivation of rhubarb in Britain, another pioneer recipe comes from 'Meg Dods'. This was the *nom de plume* of Mrs Christina Johnson whose public house at Howgate was the prototype of the Cleikum Inn which Sir Walter Scott visited with some of his friends on a boozy fishing trip to a loch in the Moorfoot Hills. In his novel *St Ronan's Well* he described it as 'used by meetings of the Helter Skelter Club and the Wildfire Club and other associations formed for the express purpose of getting rid of care and sobriety.' The Cleikum Club, of which Scott was a member, celebrated Scotland's literary heritage and was among the first of such societies to celebrate Burns' Night.

These soups are made of gourds, rhubarb, cucumbers, vegetable marrows &c. They may either be made with cream, milk or good clean gravy, and seasoned to the taste of the eater.

Peel, clean and blanch a bundle of Victorian rhubarb, cut the stems into inch lengths, and put them to a couple of quarts of good veal or beef gravy, with two or three onions, a few thin slices of bread, crust and crumb together, and salt and cayenne. Skim off all the fat and scum; simmer until tender; strain and serve on toasted sippets. This soup may be better made *maigre* with a half-pound of butter kneaded in a little flour. [The butter takes the place of sugar in modifying the tartness of the rhubarb.]

Dods 1826

Spinach and Rhubarb Soup

The late Arto Der Haroutunian, the Mancunian-Armenian architect and restaurateur whose books about Middle Eastern food have enticed many cooks and readers since their first publication, suggested that his spinach and rhubarb soup could be called *ıspanak çorbasi*, the Turkish name for a spinach, beef and tomato soup. However, the combination of spinach and rhubarb may more likely be connected to the Jewish *schav borscht* or sorrel soup, a favourite of Jews in Eastern Europe who took delight in the sharp flavour of sorrel. This, which has been called a 'mock *schav*', gets its sharpness from the rhubarb and the green colour from the spinach. Not every greengrocer stocks sorrel.

25 g / 1 oz butter
1 onion, thinly sliced
2 sticks of rhubarb, sliced
1 stick of celery, thinly sliced
1.8 litres / 3 pints water
1½ tsp salt
450 g / 1 lb fresh spinach or 225 g / 8 oz frozen
2 eggs, beaten
150 ml / ¼ pint sour cream
juice of 1 lemon
½ tsp black pepper

Melt the butter in a pan and add the onion. Fry until soft. Add the rhubarb and celery and a little water. Cover and cook until tender over a low heat. Add water and salt and bring to a brisk boil. Add the spinach. It must be washed well, and the excess water squeezed out. Cook for 15 minutes. Liquidize or sieve.

Beat the eggs, cream and lemon juice with some hot stock. Take the soup off the heat and stir in the liaison to blend it well. Add the pepper and add more salt if needed. Serve at once.

PARSNIP, RHUBARB AND GINGER SOUP

In 1998, the winner of the *Daily Telegraph* / New Covent Garden Soup Competition was Mr R. M. Austen of South Petherton in Somerset. His recipe built on Jane Grigson's winning idea of spicing up parsnips to make a wonderful winter-warmer of a soup. His recipe was subsequently published by the New Covent Garden Company in their *Soup and Beyond: Soups, Beans and Other Things* of 1999.

450 g / 1 lb parsnips, peeled and chopped
225 g / 8 oz rhubarb, chopped
1 medium onion, sliced
2 tsp root ginger, freshly grated
60 g / 2 oz butter
1 tbsp plain flour
2 tsp brown sugar
600 ml / 1 pint chicken stock
salt and pepper
fresh coriander, chopped

Cook the parsnip, rhubarb, onion and grated ginger in melted butter for 5 minutes in a covered pan. Do not let it brown. Then incorporate the flour thoroughly. Add the remaining ingredients and seasonings. Bring it to the boil, stirring constantly. Simmer gently for 15–20 minutes until cooked, then blend or sieve or mouli. Should it be too thick, ad some more stock. Sprinkle with coriander and serve.

Rhubarb, Chickpea and Mint Soup

175 g / 6 oz chickpeas or 1 can of chickpeas
175 g / 6 oz rhubarb, washed and cut into 2½ cm / 1 inch pieces
half a medium onion, chopped finely
half a stick of celery, chopped
1 tbsp olive oil
1 tsp honey
liberal squeeze of lemon juice
chicken stock
salt and pepper
2 tbsp fresh mint, chopped

Soak chickpeas in cold water overnight. Drain and cover by at least a centimetre in boiling water. Bring back to the boil. Skim any scum which rises, then cook for about 1 hour (or more if they are not this season's). Check they do not dry out. Towards the end of the cooking, add the onion and celery. Continue cooking until everything is absolutely tender. Drain, but reserve 300 ml / ½ pint of the water in which to simmer the rhubarb until it is just tender. Add back the chickpeas, celery and onion. Then add the olive oil, honey, and lemon juice. Liquidize. Add salt and pepper judiciously. Sprinkle with chopped mint.

If you use canned chickpeas, sweat the onion and celery in oil and simmer the rhubarb in chicken stock.

This makes a thick soup, which can be thinned with chicken stock or water. A few chopped almonds might also be added for texture.

CHILLED RHUBARB, GINGER
AND ELDERFLOWER SOUP

These three ingredients work well in combination. It has a flavour which is slightly heady and winy. It makes a grand opening to any meal. The suggestion comes from John Tovey's *Miller Howe Cook Book*. He was one of England's great innovators, delighting in mixing floral perfumes with savoury tastes.

175 g / 6 oz onions, peeled and finely chopped
100 g / 4 oz butter
900 g / 2 lb rhubarb, cleaned and evenly chopped
2 tablespoons of dried elderflowers or 2 heads of fresh florets
150 ml / 5 fl oz white wine
900 ml / 1½ pints milk
2 walnut-sized pieces of preserved ginger
salt and pepper
mint leaves, borage flowers or chives

Sweat the onions in the butter. Add rhubarb, elderflowers and wine. Cover and simmer gently for 45–50 minutes. Add milk and finely chopped ginger. Liquidize and sieve. Chill and adjust the seasoning. Serve garnished with mint and borage flowers. As an alternative finish, swirl in some cream and scatter chopped chives.

COLD RHUBARB SOUP

There is a strong tradition in northern and eastern Europe for fruit soups. The spring soup of Stephana Malcolm cited at the beginning of this chapter shows that Britain shared in the custom, even if by and large it disappeared from our tables in the last couple of centuries. This recipe was proposed by the founders of the Vega vegetarian restaurant where, after the Second World War, some of the most imaginative cooking in London was to be had for a very reasonable price. Subsequently, they wrote *Modern Vegetarian Cookery* (1968). In Denmark, they call this soup 'the pudding which greets the sun'.

450 g / 1 lb rhubarb
1 litre / 2 pints water
1 lemon
350 g / 12 oz sugar
25 g / 1 oz porridge oats
1 tbsp vanilla sugar
     or 25 g / 1 oz sugar and a few drops of pure vanilla essence
salt and pepper

Wipe the rhubarb and cut it into 1 cm / ½ inch pieces. Simmer in 1 pint of water. When the rhubarb is tender add the rest of the water, the juice and grated rind of the lemon, and the sugar. Bring it to the boil, add the oatflakes and simmer for 20–30 minutes. Finish with the vanilla sugar and possibly some salt and pepper as seasoning. Serve chilled.

HUNGARIAN SWEET RHUBARB SOUP
Rebarbaria Leves

Unlike the previous recipe, this soup is not cold. I first encountered it in Fred Macnicol's *Hungarian Cookery* (1978), but other versions suggest giving the dish a little spice in the form of cloves and cinnamon. In Poland, they have another cold soup where its colour is enhanced by adding strawberry jam. Of course, if the rhubarb is high summer's rather green stems, rather than champagne rhubarb or the pale pink forced rhubarb, then the colour will be a little subdued, if not subfusc.

5 tbsp sugar
salt
the rind of half a large lemon
450 g / 1 lb rhubarb
6 tbsp sour cream
30 g / 1 oz flour
1 egg yolk
6 tbsp milk

Put 1½–2 pints of water to boil with the sugar, a pinch of salt, and the grated rind of half a lemon, or somewhat more. Wash the rhubarb and wipe it. Slice it into small pieces, then add to the boiling syrup.

Slake the flour with half the cream and the milk. Add this to the rhubarb when it is nearly tender. Return to the boil and simmer for 5 minutes. Beat the egg yolk with the rest of the cream. With the soup now off the boil, add it in a thin stream to the soup, stirring it all the time.

CHAPTER FIVE

PUDDINGS

RHUBARB. –This is one of the most useful of all garden productions that are put into pies and puddings. It was comparatively little known till within the last twenty or thirty years, but it is now cultivated in almost every British garden. The part used is the footstalks of the leaves, which, peeled and cut into small pieces are put into tarts, either mixed with apples or alone. When quite young, they are much better not peeled. Rhubarb comes in season when apples are going out. The common rhubarb is a native of Asia; the scarlet variety has the finest flavour. Turkey rhubarb, the well-known medicinal drug, is the root of a very elegant plant (*Rheum palmatum*), coming to greatest perfection in Tartary. For culinary purposes, all kinds of rhubarb are the better for being blanched.

Beeton 1861, §1339

I quoted some early recipes for rhubarb tarts and rhubarb pies in the introduction. But there is, of course, an infinity of them spread across Regency and Victorian literature, each having something useful to tell us although, to be frank, the level of imaginative tinkering is not very great. The rhubarb pie given by Meg Dods in her fourth edition of 1829 reads as follows:

806. *Rhubarb-pie.* – Peel off the skin from stalks of young rhubarb, and cut them slantwise into bits of about an inch and a half. Stew them slowly in sugar, or in butter, and a little water, till soft: mash, sweeten, and make them into a covered pie or open tart. – *Obs.* Gooseberry, apple, rhubarb, and other fruit pies, eat very well cold; or the fruit may be stewed and sweetened for common

use, without further preparation. Fresh good cream is a very great improvement to all fruit pies and tarts. The next best thing is plain custard. In England the cream is often sweetened, thickened with beat yolks of eggs, and poured over the fruit. In Scotland cream for tarts is usually served either plain or merely whisked; or served over the stewed fruit whipt.

Dods goes on to suggest a delicious rhubarb pasty or turnover. In Tierra del Fuego, where soft fruit is hard to find and rhubarb has been introduced (just as in Scotland) something very similar is eaten: a rhubarb *empanada*. It is made with hot-water crust in turnover form and is remarkably similar.

816. Common apple, gooseberry, or rhubarb pasties or turnovers. – Make a hot crust with dripping or lard melting in boiling water; roll it out quickly, and cut it so as to be of a semicircular form when turned over. Lay stewed apples, rhubarb, or scalded gooseberries, in the crust, with moist sugar to sweeten; add, if apples, quince, lemon-peel, or cinnamon. Cut the edges, double up and pinch the crust, and bake the pasties in a moderate oven. If there be icing at hand they may be iced. – *Obs.* This is a cheap preparation and a greater favourite with young persons than those that are more delicate and expensive.

The Victorian royal chef Charles Francatelli was somewhat overshadowed by his more flamboyant contemporary Alexis Soyer. None the less, the rhubarb pie included in his *Plain Cookery Book for the Working Classes* (1852) is well explained and worth citing.

No. 98. Rhubarb Pie.
A bundle of rhubarb, one pound of flour, six ounces of butter, or lard, or dripping, half a pint of water, a pinch

of salt, ditto of baking-powder, eight ounces of moist sugar. First, cut up the rhubarb in pieces about an inch long, wash them in plenty of water, and drain them in a colander, or sieve. Next, place the flour in a pan, or on the table, make a hollow in the middle with your fist, place the salt and the baking-powder in it, pour in the water to dissolve them, then add the butter; mix all together by working the ingredients with the fingers of both hands, until the whole has become a firm, smooth, compact kind of paste. You now put the cleaned rhubarb into a pie-dish, with the sugar and a gill of water, roll out the paste to the exact size of the dish, and after wetting the edges of the dish all round, place the rolled-out paste upon it, and by pressing the thumb of the right hand all round the upper part of the edge, the paste will be effectually fastened on, so as to prevent the juice from running out at the sides; a small hole the size of a sixpence must be made at the top of the pie, for ventilation, or otherwise the pie would burst. Bake the pie for an hour and a quarter.

The rhubarb pie that was suggested by Mrs Annabella P. Hill in her *New Cook Book*, first published in 1867 in America, had a top and bottom crust, as well as some nice spicing that might not go amiss today. Remember that in America, the common or slang name for rhubarb was pie plant (Merriam-Webster dates its first appearance to 1838). The great cookery writer May Byron, whose *Pudding Book* and *Jam Book* are valuable compendiums of recipes and advice, comments that American pies are like our English pies in 'only one respect, the fundamental fact of being covered. Otherwise, instead of being deep, they are shallow; instead of being oval, they are round; instead of occupying pie-dishes, they are made in plates. Not seldom the under and upper crust, when baked, are slit asunder as it were a muffin, more contents inserted, and the pie-top replaced as if nothing had happened.'

596. Rhubarb Pie. – Take the tender stalks of the rhubarb; remove the skin; cut the pieces an inch long. Line the pie-plate with paste; put a layer of rhubarb and a layer of sugar, sprinkled over thick; continue this until the paste is nearly filled. Sprinkle grated lemon peel and pulverized coriander seed between each layer for flavoring; a heaped teaspoonful of flour to each pie sprinkled between the layers; add half a teacup of water; put on an upper crust, pinch the edges down carefully, and cut a slit in the centre. Bake *slowly* an hour. In all pies where there is not sufficient fruit to prevent the crust from falling in, before placing on the upper crust, cross three stout straws on the top of the pie-plate to support the crust. When the pie is done, the crust may be loosened with a pen-knife or other small instrument sufficiently to enable you to remove the straws. Tin plates are better than earthen for baking pies.

While Mrs Hill proposed lemon peel and ground coriander to season the rhubarb, an English author writing in 1874 suggested giving it some edge (as if more were needed) by adding green lime juice or 'in default of this, ... the juice of a lemon, and that of a Seville orange.' The writer of these words was the Reverend Henry Southgate, who penned *Things a Lady Would Like to Know* from his genteel home at Woodbine, Sidmouth, Devon. Another, apparently traditional, English seasoning can be made with the chopped leaves of the herb sweet cicely.

Mrs Beeton had her own rhubarb recipes, both for a tart and a pudding (the pudding one was pinched by the reverend gent. just mentioned for a ladylike dinner in April). Her tart reads like this:

RHUBARB TART.
1339. INGREDIENTS. – ½ lb. of puff-paste No. 1206, about 5 sticks of large rhubarb, ¼ lb. of moist sugar.

Mode. – Make a puff-paste by recipe No. 1206; line the edges of a deep pie-dish with it, and wash, wipe, and cut the rhubarb into pieces about 1 inch long. Should it be old and tough, string it, that is to say, pare off the outside skin. Pile the fruit high in the dish as it shrinks very much in the cooking; put in the sugar, cover with crust, ornament the edges, and bake the tart in a well-heated oven from ½ to ¾ hour. If wanted very nice, brush it over with the white of an egg beaten to a stiff froth, then sprinkle on it some sifted sugar, and put it in the oven just to set the glaze: this should be done when the tart is nearly baked. A small quantity of lemon-juice, and a little of the peel minced, are by many persons considered an improvement to the flavour of rhubarb tart.

Her boiled rhubarb pudding recalls a style of English eating that has to some extent gone out of fashion. She says this recipe will feed 6 or 7 people.

BOILED RHUBARB PUDDING.

1338. INGREDIENTS. – 4 or 5 sticks of fine rhubarb, ¼ lb. of moist sugar, ¾ lb. of suet-crust No. 1215.

Mode. – Make a suet-crust with ¾ lb. of flour, by recipe No. 1215, and line a buttered basin with it. Wash and wipe the rhubarb, and, if old, string it – that is to say, pare off the outside skin. Cut it into inch lengths, fill the basin with it, put in the sugar, and cover with crust. Pinch the edges of the pudding together, tie over it a floured cloth, put it into boiling water, and boil from 2 to 2 ½ hours. Turn it out of the basin, and serve with a jug of cream and sifted sugar.

Rhubarb and Almond Tart

I was first inspired to try this dish by a recipe from Jenny Mann's *Vegetarian Cuisine* (1982). She proposes a sort of Bakewell tart but you can go the whole hog and include the layer of jam on the bottom and the frangipane sponge filling, scattering the pieces of rhubarb to peep through the finished item. I have not given a recipe for the pastry, presuming those who do not make pastry themselves will buy a good one from the shops, or you can follow the one in the next recipe.

175 g / 6 oz sweet shortcrust pastry
1 kg / 2 lb rhubarb
castor sugar
125 g / 4 oz butter
125 g / 4 oz sugar
2 eggs, beaten
125 g / 4 oz flaked almonds

Make enough pastry to line an 8–9 inch flan case. Roll it out and line the case. Chill for 30 minutes, then trim the edge. Preheat the oven to 400°F/200°C/gas mark 6. Prick the pastry, line it with greaseproof paper and baking beans. Bake for 10 minutes, remove the beans and bake for a further 5 minutes.

Wash and wipe your rhubarb and cut into 2.5 cm/1 inch chunks. Put them in a tray, sprinkle them with castor sugar. Put them into the oven to roast until they are almost tender.

Cream the butter and sugar, then add the beaten eggs. Fold in the almonds. Arrange the rhubarb in the flan case. Pour over the sponge. Put it in an oven preheated to 180°C/350°F/gas mark 5 for 20 minutes or until the top is lightly browned.

Lattice Fruit Tart

The island of Fair Isle, midway between the Orkneys and Shetland, boasted a population of 400 at the beginning of the twentieth century. Now it is about 70 souls. That is no hindrance to their eating rhubarb. This recipe comes from the *Fair Isle Times*, the one-time community newspaper.

for the pastry
75 g / 3 oz butter
175 g / 6 oz plain flour
1 tbsp castor sugar
1 egg yolk
2 tsp water
for the filling
2 tbsp cornflour
2 tbsp castor sugar
700 g / 1½ lb rhubarb, cut into 2 cm / 1½ inch pieces
2 tbsp redcurrant jelly, warmed
for the topping
175 g / 6 oz margarine or butter, softened
35 g / 1½ oz icing sugar, sifted
175 g / 6 oz plain flour (or try replacing 2 oz flour with ground almonds)
1 tsp almond essence – less if ground almond is used.

To make the pastry, rub butter into the flour, beat the sugar with yolk and water, stir in the flour to form a soft dough. Use this to line the base and sides of a shallow oblong baking tray measuring 20 x 28 cm / 8 x 11 inches. Chill for 20 minutes.

Sprinkle the base with cornflour and sugar. Lay the rhubarb in rows on top. Brush with warmed redcurrant jelly. For the topping, beat the margarine or butter with the icing sugar. Add flour (with or without ground almonds) and essence. Spoon into a large piping bag fitted with a half-inch star tube. Pipe a lattice over the rhubarb.

Preheat the oven to 190°C/375°F/gas mark 5. Bake for 30–35 minutes. If you want to eat it now, sprinkle with sugar and cut into squares. If you wish to freeze it, you can. Wrap it well and it will keep for 6 months.

Fair Isle Times, 1 June 1984

RHUBARB, ORANGE AND ALMOND CRUMBLE PIE

A magazine recipe from the food-writer Philippa Davenport takes advantage of the perfect match of rhubarb and orange in this heart-warming pie with a crumble topping.

150 g / 5 oz unsalted butter
300 g / 10 oz plain flour
the finely grated zest of an orange
1 tsp castor sugar
2 tbsp orange juice
50 g / 2 oz flaked almonds
75 g / 3 oz pale muscovado sugar
½–1 tsp ground cinnamon
300 g / 10 oz forced rhubarb

Cut up the butter and rub it into the flour. Take 150 g / 5 oz of this mixture out of the bowl and reserve it. Stir the orange zest and castor sugar into the mixture which remains. Use the orange juice to bind it into a short-crust dough, and chill it briefly. Take a 25–30 cm / 10–12 inch fluted flan tin and line it with the pastry. Chill once again. Weigh down the base with greaseproof paper and baking beans, and bake at 200°C/400°F/gas mark 6 for 18–20 minutes, removing the paper and beans after the first 10 minutes.

Reserve a tablespoon of almonds, but crush the rest into small bits and add to the reserved flour and butter.

Make a nutty crumble by adding it to the muscovado sugar and cinnamon. Spread a third of it over the blind-baked pastry case. Then arrange the sliced rhubarb on top of this and sprinkle the remaining crumble over it. Place the pie onto a preheated baking sheet. Bake it at 200°C/400°F/gas mark 6 for 35 minutes, until the fruit is tender but not collapsing, and the crumble crisp and turning brown. Cool 5–10 minutes before serving.

Country Living, February, 1999

Cox's Orange and Rhubarb Compote

This dish should consist of Cox's Orange, or other apples which keep their shape when cooked, in a syrup of their own juices blended with rhubarb. It is delicious eaten warm with the fragrance and aroma of the apple contrasting with the sweet-sharp of the syrup. It is pleasant, if less subtle, eaten chilled with cream or with yoghurt and dark brown sugar.

450 g / 1 lb Cox's Orange apples
225 g / ½ lb young rhubarb
4 tbsp granulated sugar
4 tbsp water

Rinse your apples, quarter and core them. Slice them, not too thinly, but do not peel. Cut the wiped rhubarb stalks into 6 cm / 2.5 inch lengths. Sprinkle the sugar over the rhubarb and let it stand for 2–3 hours, then add the water and the apple slices, and cook together very gently, turning the apples in the liquid until they are tender but not mushy. Serve in small bowls.

RHUBARB AND ANGELICA

Rosemary Hemphill's handbook of herbs and spices, which was a useful guide for cooks in the 1960s, recommended stewing rhubarb with angelica leaves. This may remind the reader of an earlier suggestion we noted that sweet cicely be employed. Garden angelica, a herb of Scandinavian origin, is botanically *Angelica archangelica*. Wild angelica, *Angelica sylvestris*, is not the same thing and should not be substituted. The plant was used for its stalks and (medicinally) its roots. It seems rather apt that rhubarb, a plant most favoured in the European north, should be linked with a Scandinavian herb.

500 g / 1 lb rhubarb
300 ml / ½ pint water
100 g / 4 oz sugar
4 young angelica leaves
2 thin curls of lemon peel

Cut the rhubarb into ¾ inch lengths and put it into a pan with water, sugar, angelica leaves and lemon peel. When it has come to the boil, simmer it until tender. Remove the angelica and lemon peel. Chill and serve with yoghurt or cream.

RHUBARB AND BANANA COMPOTE

Ursula Aylmer and Carolyn McCrum's interesting book *Oxford Food, an Anthology* collects recipes from the high tables and masters' lodgings of the university. This particular combination of fruits was served at St Edmund Hall, at the Principal's table. His wife had it from her great-great-grandmother as it was made at St Vigean's manse in Arbroath. Those Scottish ministers must have been gastronomic pioneers. Rhubarb itself was relatively new and although bananas were first mentioned in English printed material in the 1630s, the fruit itself was pretty uncommon until the late Victorian period. It was virtually impossible to get the hands from their plantations to these benighted islands before they were black and fermenting.

450 g / 1 lb prepared rhubarb
75 g / 3 oz castor sugar
1 ripe banana

Wash the rhubarb and cut it into ¾ inch slices. Put it in a pan, sprinkle with sugar. Stand it for at least an hour to bring the juice out of the rhubarb. Cover it and bring it to the boil slowly and stir it gently once or twice. Turn it down and cook it gently for 2 minutes. Then turn off the heat and leave it on the stove for 5 minutes without lifting the lid, so that the rhubarb cooks but remains whole. While hot, slice the banana into the rhubarb, and serve it cold with pouring cream. If you chill it the banana will turn brown. A possible variation or injection of happy spice could be achieved by chopping up a piece of stem ginger and mixing it into the rhubarb.

Rhubarb Compote with Red Wine

There are many ways to stew rhubarb. This gives a dark syrup through which the champagne-pink nuggets will shine. The rather good cookery book writer of the turn of the last century, Lucy H. Yates, had some wise words on the difference between compotes and stewed fruit in her delightful *The Gardener and the Cook* (1912): '[The compote], which keeps the full flavour of the fruit without losing its form or spoiling its appearance, is a method to be infinitely preferred. For this you must make your syrup first by boiling together sugar and water – not too much of either; the fruit to be cooked is wiped and put in, not too much at a time, and cooked until quite tender, but not long enough to break it, and after it is done the syrup is reduced by further boiling and poured over.'

300 ml / 10 fl oz red wine
110 g / 4 oz golden castor sugar
the zest from half an orange (no pith)
the zest from half a lemon (ditto)
450 g / 1 lb forced champagne rhubarb, cut into small chunks
pinch salt

Combine the wine, sugar and citrus zest. Bring to the boil
and add the rhubarb and the salt. Cook very gently so
that the rhubarb is tender but in no way mushy. Remove
the fruit with a slotted spoon and reserve. Take out the
peels and reduce the liquid by boiling by at least one half,
adding back in any juice expressed by the rhubarb as you
go. Pour over the rhubarb and chill.

ROTE GRÜTZE

The name translates as 'red groats' and was a standby of
Schleswig-Holstein and other north German regions. In
Denmark, it is called *rødgrød*. Essentially, it was a way of
enlivening your groats (oatmeal) with the red berries of summer,
most often raspberries and redcurrants. Over time, the starch
element has changed: sago or tapioca are popular, semolina was
the favoured vehicle of East Prussian (now Poland) *Rodegrütt*, and
potato starch or cornflour were also favoured. It can be made
with rhubarb and be eaten with lashings of cream or custard, or
used as a sauce for cakes. There is little difference between this
and the Russian, Polish and Slav dish called *kissel*.

275 g / 10 oz forced rhubarb, trimmed and cut short
140 g / 5 oz raspberries
600 ml / 1 pint water
225 g / 8 oz castor sugar
vanilla pod, scraped
5 tbsp cornflour slaked in 175 ml / 6 fl oz water

Cook the rhubarb in water until soft. Add the raspberries in the last minute or two. Press them through a fine sieve and add the sugar and the scraped vanilla seeds. Cook and reduce slightly for a few minutes. Slake the cornflour and stir into the boiling pulp, cook for a minute before pouring into a large serving dish. The amount of sugar will depend on your taste, but the intention is that the mixture should not be too sweet.

RHUBARB CHARLOTTE

This recipe was collected by Margaret Costa for a book called *Food for our Times*, an anthology of recipes donated to Oxfam, which was published in 1977.

175 g / 6 oz fresh white breadcrumbs
50 g / 2 oz melted butter
450 g / 1 lb rhubarb, cut into 1 cm / ½ inch slices
50 g / 2 oz brown sugar
½ tsp ground ginger
¼ tsp each cinnamon and nutmeg
2 tbsp golden syrup
1 tbsp lemon juice

Toast the breadcrumbs in melted butter. Fill a greased china soufflé dish with alternating layers of breadcrumbs and sliced rhubarb, finishing with a layer of crumbs. Each time you spread a layer of rhubarb, sprinkle it with some of the sugar and spice mixture.

Heat the golden syrup and lemon juice in 2 tbsp water, and pour over the charlotte. Put a butter paper or some such cover over the soufflé dish and bake in a preheated oven at 200°C/400°F/gas mark 6 for 30 minutes. Then remove the cover and bake for another 10 minutes until the top is crisp and golden.

Very tough, old rhubarb may be steamed as a preliminary.

Rhubarb and Gingerbread Sponge

This recipes comes courtesy of my friend Mavis Oddie in Timaru, on the South Island of New Zealand. It is partly the coincidence that New Zealand and Australia had their strongest British connection at the moment that rhubarb was enjoying its greatest popularity, and secondarily that rhubarb fared very well in New Zealand gardens, but the fruit has always enjoyed much favour in the Antipodes.

450 g / 1 lb rhubarb
150 g / 6 oz flour
a pinch each of salt,
*   cinnamon and nutmeg*
1 tsp ground ginger
½ tsp mixed spice

100 g / 4 oz butter
50 g / 2 oz brown sugar
50 g / 2 oz golden syrup
1 egg, beaten
2 tbsp hot milk
½ tsp bicarbonate of soda

Cut the rhubarb into 2.5 cm / 1 inch pieces, and lay it in a well-greased baking dish. Sieve the flour, salt and spices together into a bowl. In a second bowl, cream the butter and sugar, then beat in the syrup. Mix well and add the beaten egg. Beat again and then fold in the dry ingredients. Lastly, stir in the hot milk with the baking soda dissolved in it. Pour this mixture over the rhubarb and bake in a preheated oven at 180°C/375°F/gas mark 5 for 35–40 minutes.

AMY'S CRUMB PIE

The delightful collection of recipes put together by Amanda Goodfellow and published by her as *A Household Legacy* in 1989 includes this 'family favourite' involving rhubarb. It certainly is enjoyable and has the advantage of being the quickest I know. I particularly like the way the unsweetened fruit contrasts with the sweet crunchy topping.

900 g / 2 lb rhubarb
ground cinnamon or grated lemon rind to taste
for the crumble topping
100 g / 4 oz butter or margarine
100 g / 4 oz plain flour
225 g / 8 oz soft brown sugar

Wipe and slice the rhubarb and put it into a greased pie dish. Strew it with the cinnamon or grated lemon. Make a coarse crumble by rubbing the butter into the flour and then mixing in the sugar. If you overwork the mixture, it will become sticky. Sprinkle it over the rhubarb evenly and pat it down lightly. Bake at 190°C/375°F/gas mark 5 for about 45 minutes, until the top is crisp and brown and the rhubarb oozing juice. Eat hot with yoghurt, crème fraîche or cream.

Rhubarb Crumble

This recipe comes from the Shetland island of Fetlar. Aptly enough, the crumble is made with oatmeal. The source of the recipe, contributed to an island fund-raising cookery book, is a lady called Adeline.

An alternative crumble, suggested by Claire Macdonald of the Kinloch Lodge Hotel on Skye, whose cookery books have kept a generation of Scottish readers well fed, is made with crumbled digestive biscuits or gingernuts. She advises that you add cinnamon to the crumble mixture and improve the rhubarb with some orange juice.

An excellent improvement proposed by the chef Sean Hill, now cooking at the Walnut Tree near Abergavenny, is that you serve a ginger custard with your crumble.

450 g / 1 lb rhubarb
50 g / 2 oz granulated sugar
75 g / 3 oz butter or margarine
75 g / 3 oz demerara sugar
100 g / 4 oz porridge oats

Wipe the rhubarb and slice it into pieces 2.5 cm / 1 inch long. Place it in layers with the granulated sugar in a greased ovenproof dish. Melt the butter and mix it well with the demerara sugar and porridge oats. Cover the fruit with the crumble mix and cook for 180°C/350°F/gas mark 4 for at least 30 minutes, until it is browned. Serve it hot or cold.

RHUBARB CLAFOUTIS

350 g / 12 oz rhubarb
300 ml / ½ pint milk, slightly warmed
25 g / 1 oz sugar
3 eggs
1 tsp vanilla extract
150 g / 6 oz plain flour
50 g / 2 oz extra sugar

Wipe the rhubarb and slice it into pieces 2.5 cm / 1 inch long. Blend together the milk, sugar, eggs, flour and vanilla until smooth. Pour some of this batter into a generous, greased pie-dish – just to cover the bottom with a 5 mm / ¼ inch layer. Preheat your oven to 180°C/ 350°F/gas mark 4. Place the dish in the oven and bake the first layer of batter until it is just set. At this point, spread the rhubarb over the surface, sprinkle with the extra sugar and pour on the remaining batter mixture. Bake for between 35 and 45 minutes, until nicely browned, and dust with sugar before serving.

This is lovely as it comes from the oven, but even better with thick, unwhipped cream. 'Delicious,' says my daughter. 'You can also make it in a single process, by first softening the rhubarb for 15 minutes in a buttered or oiled pie-dish, then pouring over the batter and sprinkling thickly with sugar. I cook it in a hot oven 200°C/400°F/gas mark 6 for more like 20 minutes – but I don't think my pie dish is as deep as was used in the original recipe. My way looks messier, but is very light.'

An alternative treatment for the rhubarb suggested by the owners of the Burrastow Hotel on Shetland is that you macerate the rhubarb for about an hour with sugar and kirsch before putting it to the batter.

Rhubarb Russe

This recipe was offered by the *Fair Isle Times* on 15 June, 1984.

450 g / 1 lb rhubarb
50 g / 2 oz granulated sugar
2 egg yolks
50 g / 2 oz castor sugar
225 ml / 8 fl oz milk
12 g / ½ oz gelatine
18 sponge fingers
the grated rind and juice of 1 orange
150 ml / 5 fl oz pint double cream, whipped
1 orange, sliced

Wipe and slice the rhubarb. Mix with the granulated sugar in a saucepan over a gentle heat until the sugar dissolves. Simmer until the fruit is tender. Put through a food mill or otherwise purée. Cool and reserve.

Cream the yolks and the castor sugar until light-coloured and creamy. Stir in the milk. Cook in a bowl over pan of boiling water till thickened. Make sure the custard never boils itself.

Whisk the gelatine into the hot custard until it is completely dissolved, then cool.

Dip the sponge fingers in orange juice. Stand them around the sides of a 1.25 litre/2.25 pint buttered soufflé dish. Mix the rest of juice, the grated rind and the rhubarb purée into the custard.

Fold in the double cream; pour into the dish; and chill until set. Now, carefully trim the protruding tops of the sponge fingers.

If you want to serve it straight away, dip the dish into hot water to turn it out. Decorate with overlapping orange slices. You can freeze this charlotte, well wrapped of course, and for best results use within 2 months.

Ruby Fruit Salad

A friend living in Tokyo, Susan Ugawa, sent me this recipe. She advises using red-stemmed rhubarb. The salad usefully turns small quantities of fruit from your own garden into a stunning looking dish with a fresh flavour. If your children have grown the raspberries and strawberries, and there aren't enough to go round the family, this will make the most of them. It is also easy enough to be made by the children themselves, though the amount of fruit might diminish in the making.

350 g / 12 oz prepared rhubarb cut in 2 cm / ¾ inch lengths
100 g / 4 oz granulated sugar
225 g / 8 oz raspberries
225 g / 8 oz strawberries
3 tbsp water

Put the rhubarb in a saucepan with the sugar and water. Bring to the boil and simmer until barely tender, stirring continuously – this will take only a few minutes. Add the raspberries and cook for a further few minutes. Turn into a serving dish and add the strawberries when the cooked fruit becomes cooler. Chill well before serving with whipped cream.

Just before serving, a little whisky or brandy may be stirred in.

Rhubarb Cranachan

A fund-raising pamphlet for Sand Church was the source of this recipe. The parish church in the westside of Shetland is the smallest on the island. My daughter, who tested the instructions, put some of the sugar with the oatmeal or sesame and grilled them together. It can also be made with whipping cream and Greek yoghurt. A classic cranachan or cream-crowdie will take its sweetness from heather honey, and spice things up a little with whisky or Drambuie.

450 g / 1 lb rhubarb, wiped and cut into pieces
1–2 tbsp granulated sugar, to taste
50 g / 2 oz medium oatmeal or sesame seeds
300 ml / 10 fl oz double cream
150 ml / 5 fl oz fromage frais
25–50 g castor sugar

Stew the rhubarb, adding sugar to taste. Toast oatmeal or sesame seeds under a preheated grill until lightly browned. Whisk cream until it is holding its shape. Fold in the fromage frais, sugar and all but two tablespoons of the oatmeal or sesame seeds. Layer the rhubarb and cream mixture, then sprinkle over the remaining oatmeal or sesame seeds.

Sandsting Specials

RHUBARB MERINGUE

The idea of rhubarb meringue has been around for some time. May Byron had a recipe in her *Pudding Book* (1917) which entailed blind-baking a crust over an upside-down pie-plate then filling the cooled shell with fruit topped with meringue. It went like this:

Bake the crust on an inverted pie-plate. To prepare the filling, cut the rhubarb into inch lengths, put a layer into a saucepan, and sprinkle with sugar; add other layers of rhubarb and sugar, and cook till tender, using one cup of sugar to each pound of rhubarb. To each scant pint of cooked rhubarb add the juice of half a lemon and the well-beaten yolks of two eggs; pour the mixture into the baked crust, and set in the oven until the eggs have thickened the mixture. Spread a meringue made of the two whites of eggs over the top of the rhubarb, and brown delicately in the oven.

Lydia Strong, in a fund-raising cookery book for St Andrew's Church in Penrith, Cumbria (which has a most amazing eighteenth-century interior, designed by Nicholas Hawksmoor in 1720), made the following proposal for a rhubarb meringue without the pastry case.

450 g / 1 lb rhubarb
the grated rind and the juice of an orange
2 eggs, separated
100 g / 4 oz sugar
35 g / 1½ oz cornflour

Cut up the rhubarb and put it in a greased dish with the grated orange rind. Put the juice in a pot with enough water to make 15 fl oz. Mix 50 g / 2 oz sugar and cornflour, slake with the liquid and heat. Stir until thick. Let it cool. Add the beaten yolks. Pour this over the rhubarb. Preheat your oven to 170°C/325°F/gas mark 3 and bake for 20 minutes. Whisk the whites until stiff, then fold in the rest of the sugar. Spread over the rhubarb and continue to cook (for about 20 minutes) until the meringue has browned on its peaks.

St. Andrew's Recipe Book 2004

Nancy's Rhubarb and Yoghurt Fool

This recipe is another from New Zealand. The authors estimate it will serve eight people.

500 g / 1 lb prepared rhubarb
60 g / 2 oz castor sugar
200 ml / 7 fl oz plain yoghurt
300 ml / ½ pint double cream
dark chocolate or crystallized ginger

Cut the rhubarb into small pieces and place in an ovenproof dish with 30 g / 1 oz of castor sugar and the butter and cook until tender. Purée in a blender.

Beat the yoghurt and cream with 30 g castor sugar until slightly thicker than the purée. Mix all together gently. Pour into dessert glasses and chill. Decorate with grated chocolate or finely chopped ginger.

'A refreshing, simple but glamorous dessert.'

Mary Browne, Helen Leach and Nancy Titchbourne 1980

BURNT RHUBARB AND ORANGE CREAM

This recipe can be made with thick Greek yoghurt or with whipped cream. If the latter, less is required. I like to make this a day in advance. It does not separate out.

125 g / 4 oz rhubarb, wiped and chopped small
50 g / 2 oz granulated sugar
the grated rind and the juice of an orange
300 ml / 8 oz Greek yoghurt or 150 ml / 4 oz cream
muscovado sugar

Put the rhubarb and half the sugar in an oven-proof dish and sprinkle it with a dessertspoon of the orange juice; cover and cook in a lowish oven until tender. Cool and spoon off as much of the liquid that will have come out of the fruit to make up 50–75 ml when added to the remaining orange juice. Place the remaining sugar in a medium-sized saucepan, about 7 inches across, and heat it until it caramelizes. Immediately add about two-thirds of the liquid, stirring vigorously, and reduce it for about two minutes over a lowered heat. Watch for splashes and splatters. Cool this caramel and add the grated rind to it. Fold the rhubarb pulp and then the burnt orange gently into the yoghurt or whipped cream. Aim to distribute the pulp and the orange through the mixture without homogenizing it, so that it is instead streaky. Dish into four small bowls and sprinkle with muscovado sugar.

Something of the same idea, but different of course, can be found in a book by Caroline Waldegrave, Puff Fairclough and Janey Orr called *Leith's Easy Dinners*, a useful compendium from the cookery school of that name. Here the rhubarb is stewed with some orange peel and orange flower water, then shared between ramekins, topped with dark brown sugar and grated orange rind, and finished with Greek yoghurt and cream.

CAIRGEIN WITH RHUBARB

Cairgein is the Gaelic word for the seaweed known elsewhere as Irish moss or carrageen. I found the recipe in a publicity leaflet put out by a North Uist company, Hebridean Health Ltd. Carrageen has the ability to set food, much like agar-agar which comes from a related seaweed. It has often been favoured by vegetarians. The recipe does not give much idea of how to deal with the cairgein. It can be bought ready to cook in packs of about 25 g or 1 oz. First you soak it in cold water until it is soft, then simmer it in the water as in the recipe for about 20 minutes before straining it into the fruit purée.

500 g / 1 lb rhubarb, wiped and sliced
600 ml / 1 pint water
ginger or cloves
sugar and honey to taste
7 g / 2 tsp cairgein

Put the rhubarb in a small amount of the water and add flavourings such as cloves or ginger according to taste. Cook until broken down into a purée.

Simultaneously soak the cairgein in cold water. Then use the rest of the water to simmer it for 20 minutes. Strain it into the rhubarb. Mix thoroughly, and add sugar or honey according to taste. Put it in a mould that has been rinsed in cold water and chill until it is set (about 3 hours).

This use of seaweed to set a mould finds an echo in a vegetarian recipe book emanating from a holiday hotel or guest-house called Penlee in the South Devon village of Stoke Fleming that catered for the *bien pensant*, vegetarian and left-wing élite of Britain in the early years of the twentieth century. It is surprising how often the place crops up in the memoirs of old Labour politicians: sandals and short trousers by the seaside. The noted architect Clough Williams-Ellis (creator of Portmeirion) designed alterations to the house at Penlee.

1 ½ pounds of rhubarb, weighed after trimming
¾ pound of loaf sugar
half a lemon
½ ounce of agar-agar
1 gill of water
a little carmine [cochineal]

METHOD. – Wipe the rhubarb and cut it into pieces about ½ inch long. Put it in a Welbank or casserole with the grated lemon-rind, sugar, and half the water. Stew gently until tender, then rub through a fine wire sieve. Cut up the agar-agar and boil in the rest of the water. Strain it into the rhubarb-pulp, adding a few drops of carmine to colour. Rinse out the mould with cold water, pour in the rhubarb, and leave until it is cold. Serve with boiled custard.

Rhubarb makes a sensational jelly. Its delicately pink hues sparkle and glow in the soft light of the dinner table. It is possible to make the jelly clear by stewing champagne rhubarb and straining off the juice which can then be set with gelatine. Alternatively, a mould filled with the rhubarb pieces themselves can be set and turned out wobbling onto a dish. May Byron suggests you do it this way:

Rhubarb Jelly (Plain)

Cut one pound of rhubarb into inch-lengths, place in a baking-dish in alternate layers with sugar (one breakfastcupful will suffice). Add one cupful of cold water, the thinly peeled rind of one lemon, and a little syrup of preserved ginger or a small piece of root-ginger. Bake until the rhubarb is tender but not broken. Remove the rind and root. Soak one ounce of gelatine in half a cupful of cold water and stand this in hot water till it dissolves. Strain it into the rhubarb, add juice of one lemon, and pour into a wetted mould, a little at a time, letting [it] set a little before adding more, otherwise the rhubarb will all sink to the bottom.

Rhubarb Jelly (Very Clear)

The Cookery Book of Lady Clark of Tillypronie, arranged and edited by Catherine Frances Frere and published in 1909, is a treasure-trove of late-Victorian kitchen lore and remarkably comprehensive in its range. Her recipe for a clear rhubarb jelly (not the fruit-filled one given above) is full of sound advice. The recipe was given to Lady Clark, the book records, by one Mrs Brinkler in 1883.

Do not spare the rhubarb as the juice only is used.

Stew the rhubarb in but little water, as it is in itself three parts water. Strain two or three times through a jelly-bag till the juice runs quite clear, and use 1 white of egg to clarify it. Add, for 1 qt. of jelly ½ lb. of sugar, and 1 ½ ozs. of gelatine. If you want colour, add 3 drops of cochineal. If you bury the jelly in ice, use less gelatine. (1 oz. of gelatine *very much iced* is enough for a mould.)

You pour the jelly into a ring mould and put it on the ice, and you fill the hollow centre of the jelly before serving, with Chantilly cream flavoured with pounded vanilla.

(For stewed rhubarb, or for tarts, should the acid be objected to, first boil the rhubarb in water, and *throw that water away*; finish in fresh water, and do not sweeten the rhubarb till you use this second water.)

RHUBARB GINGER CRUNCH

In June 1984, *The Fair Isle Times* was waxing lyrical about rhubarb. I have already given you their lattice fruit tart, but two weeks later, the editor saw fit to print this proposal for rhubarb ginger crunch.

The name raises the vexed question of the precise identity of all these crunches, crumbles, cobblers, bettys and crisps (and if you are American, slumps, pandowdys and grunts for good measure). The crunch we're dealing with here reminds me of those 1950s cheesecake recipes that depended on a crust of crushed biscuits. In some respects, too, it is rather like a crumble pie with its top and bottom layers. Some crunches are not made with biscuit but rather with oatmeal.

For a handy shorthand, crumbles are topped with a crumbly pastry mixture and sometimes with oatmeal; cobblers are a fruit stew with dumplings made of biscuit dough; a crisp is pretty much like a crumble but made with a streusel dough (this the *Oxford Companion to Food* would claim to be the Central European original of the crumble topping, made with more sugar and less flour; crumbles, the *Companion* remarks, are a twentieth-century phenomenon). A betty is made up of layers of baked fruit and breadcrumbs; a crunch is a crumble with two layers of crumb (whether biscuit or oatmeal) sandwiching the fruit filling. Grunt, pandowdy and slump are American 'spoon pies': grunts are steamed; slumps can be steamed or baked. Pandowdys would appear to be a pie with a broken crust made from biscuit dough.

300 g / 10 oz gingernuts, crushed
100 g / 4 oz butter, melted
350 g / 12 oz rhubarb, prepared
100 g / 4 oz castor sugar
1 tbsp water
2 eggs, separated
200 g / 8 oz cream cheese
2 tbsp ginger jam
12 g / ½ oz gelatine dissolved in a tbsp hot water, cooled
150 ml / 5 fl oz double cream
1 piece stem ginger, sliced

Mix the biscuits and the butter. Press half of this mixture firmly into the base of a greased 10 cm / 8 inch loose-bottomed tin. Chill.

Gently heat the rhubarb, sugar and water until boiling. Simmer until syrupy. Purée. Cool. Beat the egg yolks, cream cheese and ginger jam until smooth; then add the rhubarb and the softened gelatine. Whip the double cream to a soft peak and fold into your mixture. Whisk the egg whites until stiff and fold these in. Pour all this on to the crumb base. Chill until set.

Sprinkle with the remaining crumbs, pressing them on lightly so as not to damage the filling. Remove the cake carefully from the tin. Decorate with stem ginger.

Fair Isle Times, 15 June 1984

Rhubarb Fool (1)

This may perhaps be the first port of call to a rhubarb pudding-maker. It captures almost to perfection the evanescent flavour of the stalks, and imparts a creamy richness to their eating. It is also extremely simple.

500 g / 1 lb forced rhubarb, cut into short lengths
1 tbsp orange flower water
the grated rind of half an orange
60 g / 2 oz vanilla sugar
225 ml / 8 fl oz whipping cream

Cook the rhubarb with the orange flower water and the sugar over a low heat until tender. Drain and leave to cool. Whip the cream until stiff and fold in the fruit. Serve in glasses.

A bolder recipe, which is expressed merely in terms of ratios, can be used whatever the quantity of rhubarb you may have.

Rhubarb Fool (2)

Wipe and trim the rhubarb. Cut into short lengths and weigh it. Add half its weight in castor sugar. Cook in a heavy-bottomed, covered pan, slowly. Put through the blender. Season with grated orange rind. Cool. Measure the resulting purée and add half its volume in Jersey cream. Whisk, but do not over whisk.

Rhubarb Fool (3)

An almost identical recipe from the same household has a scantier proportion of sugar and rather more cream. These alternatives may be deployed at different times of the season, depending on the tartness or delicacy of the rhubarb.

In this one, clean and cut up rhubarb. Cook with 100 g / 4 oz sugar to each 450 g / 1 lb of rhubarb and a little grated orange rind until tender. Do not add water. Put through the blender. Cool. Mix with an equal amount of double cream. Whisk till thick.

Rhubarb Flummery

The original flummery (perhaps deriving from the Welsh word *llymru*) was a dish of oatmeal that had been long soaked in water and which was then cooked until almost solid. A sort of thick porridge. It was eaten with honey, and sometimes given a kick with wine or beer. In Georgian times, it changed, it was still fairly solid, but it was cream or ground almonds set with a calf's foot or hartshorn, a kind of blancmange. In America, the word continued in use longer than here in Britain and came to be a dish of fruit thickened with cornflour. The author May Byron, writing during the First World War, offered English housewives this flummery of rhubarb (using the term in an American way).

Cut up one pound of rhubarb, steam it till tender in a stone jar. Dissolve two ounces of gelatine in a little cold water, add this to the rhubarb with four tablespoonfuls of sugar. Mix all well and pass through a sieve. Pour into a lined pan with one teacupful of cream, and stir until the flummery heats through. It must not boil. Just before turning it into a glass dish, stir in one teaspoonful of essence of lemon. Let it grow cold before serving.

RHUBARB MOUSSE

This is a desperation pudding for people in isolated places. Neighbours are coming for dinner? Well, there is always rhubarb – but they have rhubarb in the garden too and you both keep hens. How to produce something different? The contents of the store cupboard have to be raided. I found the recipe as a contribution from Jene Pitaluga to *A Taste of the Falkland Islands*, a little book published in 1989. It's somehow comforting to think of rhubarb growing by the southern ocean as well as in the northern waters that lap the coasts of Shetland.

1 packet raspberry or blackcurrant jelly
300 ml / ½ pint boiling water
450 g / 1 lb cooked and sweetened rhubarb
150 ml / 5 fl oz double cream
2 egg whites stiffly beaten
Cream and chocolate curls to decorate

Dissolve the jelly in the boiling water and leave to cool. Add the cooked rhubarb to the cooled but not yet set jelly and blend it until the volume has increased. Turn into a bowl and stir in the cream. Fold in the beaten egg whites. Pour into a bowl or individual dishes and decorate when set with cream or chocolate curls to taste.

'THAT RHUBARB DESSERT'

Sometimes a recipe conjures up its own setting. I found myself imagining a family reunion of many sisters. It is approaching its end, and the family are a little lethargically settled in the living-room of the holiday cottage around a good fire. There are always good fires in my ideal houses – perhaps because there always were in my childhood. Someone must go and do something about dinner, everyone is reluctant to brave the cold kitchen. The first course is alright but... 'Oh, use your imagination,' the youngest sister, pushed half-protesting into the kitchen, was told when she asked about the pudding.

Andreena Teed, a Shetland exile in Canada, wrote to me, 'Someone made this one evening a few years ago when there was not enough stewed rhubarb or apple sauce to go around, but mixed together made a substantial quantity, especially when mixed with whipped cream. It was an instant success.'

A good left-overs recipe for the ad hoc feeding of a small multitude, it is infinitely extendable. Its success will depend on tasting as you mix to get the right balance of the ingredients, basic as they are.

500–750 g / 1–1 ½ lb stewed rhubarb
500–750 g / 1–1 ½ lb apple sauce (i.e. stewed apples slightly
*   sweetened)*
250 ml of whipped cream

Add extra sugar or lemon juice if desired

CHAPTER SIX

RHUBARB CAKES

A health warning from a great cook:

We have inserted here but a comparatively limited number of receipts for this 'sweet poison', as they have been emphatically called. And we would willingly have diminished even further the space which has been allotted to them, that we might have had room in their stead for others of a more useful character; but we have been reluctant to withdraw such a portion of any of the chapters as might affect materially the character of the work, or cause dissatisfaction to any of our kind readers.

Eliza Acton 1845

MOIST ALMOND RHUBARB CAKE
WITH WALNUTS AND ORANGE

225 g / 8 oz rhubarb
25 g / 1 oz sugar
225 g / 8 oz wholemeal flour
1 tsp baking powder
75 g / 3 oz walnuts roughly chopped
1 tsp grated nutmeg
75 g / 3 oz ground almonds
the grated rind and juice of 1 large orange
175 g / 6 oz demerara sugar
85 ml / 3 fl oz sunflower oil
2 eggs

Cut the rhubarb up finely, add 25 g / 1 oz sugar, and put it aside so that the rhubarb absorbs the sugar. Stew gently, purée it and then cool it. Meanwhile, grease a 10 cm / 8 inch cake tin and line with oiled greaseproof paper.

Combine the wholemeal flour, baking powder, chopped walnuts, nutmeg, ground almonds and the grated orange rind. In a large bowl, cream together the sugar and oil and beat in the eggs one by one. Stir in the dry ingredients, the orange juice and 3 tbsp of the rhubarb purée to make a soft dough. Turn it into the cake tin and sprinkle it with sugar. Bake in an oven preheated to 170°C/325°F/gas mark 3 for about 45 minutes to 1 hour, testing with a skewer to check it is cooked through.

HJÓNABANDSSAELA

The name means 'Happy marriage' in Icelandic and the recipe was given me by Kristin Pétersdóttir, a visitor to Shetland.

225 g / 8 oz margarine or butter
250 g / 9 oz sugar
350 g / 12 oz flour
175 g / 6 oz porridge oats
1 tsp bicarbonate of soda
1 egg
rhubarb jam

Everything but the jam goes into a bowl and gets kneaded together. Divide into three parts. Two should be rolled out, and cut to fit into two shallow round cake tins. The jam should be spread over them. The third part of the dough is cut into strips which are put around the edge of each cake. Any left over should be used to decorate the tops. Bake in a moderate oven, about 160°C/320°F/gas mark 3, for about 30 minutes. Even Icelanders have been known to say this can be quite a dry mouthful. Try it, therefore, with cream on top.

Randalín or Vínaterta

Had she wished, Kristin Pétersdóttir could also have given me this recipe, an Icelandic standby (very popular too among Icelanders who have settled in Canada) that deploys lashings of rhubarb jam. The word *randalín* means 'striped lady', while *vínaterta* means 'Viennese torte'. Scandinavians are keen to ascribe much fine pastry work to Vienna. The original recipe for this cake included an amount of hartshorn or baker's ammonia. This was a widely used raising agent in Scandinavia and is said to impart tremendous crispness and lightness to biscuit doughs. I have substituted baking powder.

> *500 g / 1 lb flour*
> *250 g / 8 oz sugar*
> *1 ½ tsp baking powder*
> *a pinch of ground cardamom*
> *250 g / 8 oz margarine or butter, softened*
> *2 eggs*

Mix together all the dry ingredients. Add the margarine or butter, kneading until well mixed. Cool in the refrigerator for 12–24 hours. Divide into three parts and roll out into discs of approximately 1–1.5 cm / ½ inch thickness. Try to keep each part the same shape, size and thickness as the others. Lay them out on a large greased baking sheet.

Preheat the oven to 200°C/400°F/gas mark 6. Bake until golden in colour and done through. This needs careful watching. Remove from the oven and allow to cool. When the cake is almost cold, spread rhubarb jam on top of two of the layers and sandwich them together.

RUSSIAN RHUBARB CAKE

Another idea from northern climes is one given by George and Cecilia Scurfield in their little book of cake recipes, *Homemade Cakes and Biscuits*, first published in 1963. They were a remarkable couple, social activists (particularly on behalf of country folk), pioneer retailers (perhaps an inspiration for Habitat), early advocates of home-baking, and much more. I have suggested that the cake mixture might contain orange, in counterpoint to the rhubarb.

350 g / 12 oz self-raising flour
3 tsp baking powder
4 eggs
250 g / 9 oz butter, softened
250 g / 9 oz castor sugar
6 tbsp milk
grated rind of 2 oranges
9 sticks rhubarb (enough for 3 cups), chopped
demerara sugar

Sift the flour and baking powder into a bowl, then add all the other ingredients except the rhubarb and demerara. Beat well for 2 minutes. Line a large roasting tray with baking paper or foil. Spread the cake mixture over the whole, then top with the chopped rhubarb which you sprinkle generously with brown sugar. Preheat your oven to 200°C/400°F/gas mark 6 and bake for about 45 minutes.

RHUBARB AND BANANA CAKE

This recipe was kindly given me by Naomi Graham of Hove.

125 g / 5 oz butter
2 small cups brown sugar
2 eggs
2 cups flour
1 tsp bicarbonate of soda
pinch of salt
1 cup of milk
1 cup of chopped rhubarb and ½ cup of sliced banana
 – alternatively 1½ cups of rhubarb
1 tsp vanilla essence
1 tbsp lemon juice

Topping
¼ cup granulated sugar
1 tsp cinnamon
½ cup walnuts, chopped
1 tsp melted butter

Cream the butter and sugar, add eggs and beat well. Sift flour with soda and salt, and add to the butter cream alternately with the milk. Add the chopped rhubarb, banana, vanilla and lemon juice, folding them in well. Put into a large and deep, greased and floured 22 cm / 9 inch cake tin. Top the cake with the sugar mixed with cinnamon, nuts and butter. Bake in a preheated oven at 180°C/350°F/gas mark 4 for 40–45 minutes. Leave in the cake tin at least 30 minutes before turning out. Treat as an upside-down cake. This is a cake to eat fresh, even slightly warm.

RHUBARB GINGERBREAD

This is dark and moist with gooey rhubarb in the middle. It will feed a large crowd. The combination of rhubarb and ginger is much appreciated so how suitable, therefore, that the fruit should be absorbed into Britain's favourite festive cake. Josceline Dimbleby's pudding book was a *vade mecum* for thousands during the 1970s; she has an excellent version. A more recent writer, Annie Bell, whose recipes have been greatly appreciated by the current generation of home cooks, has also explored the possibilities.

110 g / 4 oz soft brown sugar
110 g / 4 oz unsalted butter
225 g / 8 oz black treacle
225 g / 8 oz plain flour
1 level tsp bicarbonate of soda
50 g / 2 oz crystallized ginger, chopped finely
1 tsp ground ginger
2 eggs, lightly whisked
4 tbsp milk
225 g / 8 oz rhubarb chopped into small pieces

Melt the sugar, butter and treacle over a low heat, beating well. Sieve together the flour and bicarbonate, add the gingers. Add the sugar mixture and beat well. Beat in the eggs and the milk. Stir the pieces of rhubarb into the cake mixture and put into a buttered 30.5 cm / 12 inch loaf tin, the bottom lined with baking parchment. Preheat the oven to 170°C/325°F/gas mark 3 and bake for about 30 minutes. Then turn the oven to 150°C/300°F/ gas mark 2, cover the gingerbread with a piece of foil and bake for another 30 minutes until the skewer comes out clean on testing. The top may be dusted with icing sugar.

Annie Bell, drawing on an idea from the Scottish writer Susan Lawrence, works a variation on this in her *Gorgeous Cakes* whereby she bakes a gingerbread, splits it in half and fills the sandwich with a thick and luscious rhubarb fool.

RHUBARB, ALMOND AND LEMON CAKE

I make no apology for using a microwave for part of the preparation. It is not, however, essential and the lemon can be cooked on the stove. My recipe was published in *Shetland Life*, no. 319, May 2007.

6 sticks rhubarb (enough for 2 cups), chopped
220 g / 8 oz soft brown sugar
half a lemon
2 large duck eggs or 3 large hens' eggs
100 g / 4 oz ground almonds
60 g / 2 oz wholemeal or white self-raising flour
½ tsp ground cardamom
1 tsp ground ginger
plain yoghurt

Put the rhubarb in a pan with about one third of the sugar and put in a warm place until the juices start to run and the sugar dissolves. Chop the lemon roughly, rind and all, and microwave it (covered) in about a cup of water at half power for 10 minutes until softened. Put the rhubarb on to cook until the juices are beginning to caramelize, then take off the heat. Blitz the lemon with a hand blender or in a food processor. Line a small cake tin with greaseproof or baking parchment.

Whisk the eggs with the remainder of the sugar until pale and creamy. Now stir in gently the ground almonds, the flour, the blitzed lemon and the spices. Don't beat it too vigorously, and add a little yoghurt to loosen the texture if it's a little stiff. Pour the mixture into the cake tin and spoon the rhubarb and juices over the top. Cook in a moderate oven (180°C/350°F/gas mark 4) for about an hour until a skewer comes out clean. The fruit will sink slightly into the cake as it cooks. Cover the cake with foil or a lid if it begins to brown. Cool it in the tin before turning out.

AMERICAN RHUBARB BREAD

This recipe was given me by Jenni Simmons, formerly of Shetland.

¾ cup runny honey
½ cup of vegetable oil
1 egg
225 g / 8 oz flour
1 small cup of buttermilk (milk soured with lemon juice, at a
  pinch)
2½ tsp baking soda
½ tsp salt
4 sticks rhubarb (enough for 1½ cups) cut into small squares
60 g / 2 oz (½ cup) chopped nuts (optional)
vanilla essence, or the seeds scraped from a vanilla pod
for the topping
100 g / 3 oz (½ cup) brown sugar blended with
  1 tsp cinnamon
  1½ tsp butter

Mix honey and oil, and add the egg. Beat well. Sift the flour, then add the honey-oil mixture alternately with buttermilk and soda and salt. Stir in the rhubarb, vanilla and nuts. Put it in two small well-greased loaf tins or one large one. Spread with the topping mixture. Preheat the oven to 180°C/350°F/gas mark 4 and bake for between 45 and 60 minutes. The top should feel firm yet springy. Leave in the tins for 10 minutes, then cool on a wire rack.

DATE AND RHUBARB SQUARES

The cookbook by Roberta Longstaff and Dr Jim Mann called *The Healthy Heart Diet Book* offers recipes that are sugar-free and not too injurious to the heart. The somewhat aetiolated nature of the ingredients may alarm some of us, but this is a useful sugarless cake, and quick to make. Sweetness comes from the dates. Those with healthy hearts may like to put them at risk by adding a finely chopped lump or two of preserved ginger, and sprinkling the top with sugar.

225 g / 8 oz rhubarb cut into 1.5 cm / ½ inch pieces
225 g / 8 oz wholemeal flour
3 tsp baking powder
50 g / 2 oz polyunsaturated margarine
170 g / 6 oz stoneless dates, chopped
1 egg, beaten
4 tbsp of skimmed milk

Put the prepared rhubarb to cook in a small amount of water for about 5 minutes, stirring it gently from time to time, then drain it. Mix the flour and baking powder in a largish bowl. Rub in the margarine, so that the mix looks like fine breadcrumbs. Add the chopped dates and rhubarb and stir well. Now add the beaten egg and milk and stir. Put it in a 10 cm / 8 inch square non-stick cake tin. Preheat the oven to 190°C/375°F/gas mark 5 and bake for 30–45 minutes. When cool, cut it into squares.

Rhubarb Muffins

I began to bake muffins using Cathy Prange and Joan Pauli's *Muffin Mania* as my guide. The authors were sisters in Kitchener, Ontario who published their book themselves in 1982, kicking off an amazing best-seller which in Canada outsold most other cookbooks of the decade. Joan Pauli died in 1992 and the book went out of print in 1997 having sold more than half a million copies. It is now published once more by Cathy Prange's granddaughter. A heartwarming tale. They called their rhubarb muffin 'Winnie's Rhubarb Muffin'.

150 g / 6 oz plain flour
1 ½ tsp baking powder
100 g / 4 oz sugar
120 ml / 4 fl oz milk
60 ml / 2 fl oz sunflower oil
½ tsp vanilla essence or a few drops almond essence
4 sticks rhubarb (enough for 1½ cups) cut into small squares
1 large egg
castor sugar for the top

Sift flour and baking powder together, add the sugar, then beat in the milk, oil, egg and flavouring. Add the prepared rhubarb and stir again. Spoon into 6 muffin pans or cases. Preheat the oven to 190°C/375°F/gas mark 5. Sprinkle with castor sugar before baking then cook for about 30 minutes.

WHOLEMEAL RHUBARB BUNS

*150 g / 6 oz prepared rhubarb in ½ inch dice (use a bright red
    rhubarb if possible)*
225 g / 8 oz wholemeal flour
1 tsp baking powder
½ tsp ground cinnamon
150 g / 6 oz butter or margarine
1 large egg
60 g / 2 oz raw sugar

Wipe and dice very small the rhubarb. Reserve. Sift
the flour, baking powder and spice together. Rub in the
butter, then add the beaten egg. Stir well, and add the
raw sugar and rhubarb and mix thoroughly. Grease a
baking tray and put dessertspoonfuls of the mixture on
it. Sprinkle with white sugar. Bake in a preheated oven
at 190°C/375°F/gas mark 5 for approximately 25 minutes.
Cool on a rack. This makes about 18 buns.

CHAPTER SEVEN

RHUBARB ICES

Mrs A.B. Marshall was the Empress of Ice-cream. Her book *Fancy Ices* popularized it in Victorian England when rhubarb was fashionable. A well-known variety of rhubarb was called after the Queen, and another after Prince Albert. She was certainly a thrusting business woman. Not only did she publish cookery books, but she ran a cookery school. The end-papers of her books promote every form of kitchen ware and larder supply, the advertisements reinforced by the wording and make-up of her recipes. Her entry in the *Oxford Dictionary of National Biography* gives a fascinating account of her business activities.

Sorbet de Rhubarbe de Nantes

Put in a stewpan two pounds of well-washed rhubarb cut up small, one pint of water, six ounces of loaf sugar, the peel of one lemon, two bay leaves, and sufficient of Marshall's Liquid Carmine to make it a nice red colour; bring it to the boil, let it simmer till tender, then rub it through a clean tammy cloth, and when it is cool flavour it with half a pint of claret and a wineglass of "Silver Rays" rum. Freeze it in the charged ice machine to semi-solid consistency, dish it in prepared ice-water cups (see recipe), place in each one or two pieces of preserved or crystallized ginger ... and serve one to each person after the remove. These may also be served for a dessert.

Ice-water cups: fill the ice-water cups three-parts full of plain or coloured cold water; fix on the covers and put the moulds on the bottom of the charged ice-cave for two and a half to three hours; then take up, dip each shape separately into cold water, and turn out the cups onto a clean dry cloth, and use for a sorbet, or they can also be filled with custard or fruit ices if liked.

Mrs A.B. Marshall 1894

She does not mention that when the sorbet has reached a mushy state it should be beaten and then refrozen. Before serving it should be moved from the freezer to the refrigerator for half an hour. The alcohol may be replaced by Ribena if it is to be served to children. No other colouring will be needed.

I have never seen Marshall's ice-water cups, which were made of metal, but I have used two bowls of different sizes to make a large ice-bowl. Put a little water in the larger bowl to a depth of about three-quarters of an inch. Put it in the freezer. When it has frozen, centre the smaller bowl in it. Add a little water in the gap between the two bowls and re-freeze. Then pour water in the gap between the two bowls until the gap is about three quarters full. Unmould by immersing the two bowls in cool water. Store the ice-bowl in the freezer until needed. I used Pyrex bowls very successfully for some time, and then the larger one cracked. The ice had expanded. Hence I suggest metal bowls.

In a later and simpler book, *The Book of Ices*, Mrs Marshall had instructions for making a rhubarb ice-cream.

52. – RHUBARB CREAM ICE
(*Crème de Rhubarbe*)

Make this as for gooseberry cream ice (No. 32), using good ripe rhubarb; colour with Marshall's carmine, and use for suppers, tennis parties, etc.

32. – GOOSEBERRY CREAM ICE
(*Crème de Groseilles Vertes*)

Put one quart of gooseberries on the stove in a pan, with half a pint of water, 6 ounces of castor sugar; boil, and when cooked pass through the tammy. If green berries, use a little sap green, or apple green to colour; if red, a little carmine or cherry red. When tammied, mix with a pint of sweetened cream or custard, and freeze. Serve for dessert.

Mrs A.B. Marshall n.d.

Rhubarb and Strawberry Ice-cream

To me this ice-cream is the very essence of summer, and I'd like to call it Summertime, but no-one would know what I meant, and when I started, 'Take two cups of finely-sliced rhubarb,' no-one would believe me. So...

The combination of strawberries and rhubarb is much favoured by modern recipe-writers, with plenty of cakes, cobblers, puddings and pies. Raspberries, too, get some support; although I must admit that often mixtures only succeed in detracting from the perfection of each part.

I have included in my method below instructions for making ice-cream without a machine. However, nowadays many people own gadgets that either work inside the freezer or are self-contained, both freezing and churning. The recipes quoted from Mrs Marshall reflect her advocacy and manufacture of pioneer (manual) ice-cream makers.

A pleasing curlicue to this recipe is to add fresh mint.

6 sticks red rhubarb (enough for 2 cups), finely chopped
1 cup of white sugar
2 punnets (2 ½ cups) hulled strawberries
300 ml / 10 fl oz whipping cream
2 egg whites

Sprinkle the finely chopped rhubarb with the sugar, and let it stand for 6 hours. Cook very gently (adding no water) until it is soft. Cut the hulled strawberries in halves or quarters, depending on their size, and add to the rhubarb. Bring the mixture to the boil, and turn down. Remove as soon as the strawberries have heated right through. Cool somewhat, then give the mixture a brief whirl in the blender. It should not be too smooth. Chill.

Whip the cream just short of stiffness and fold it into the fruit mixture. Place it in the freezer in a metal tray until it starts thickening. Then stir in very thoroughly two whipped egg whites and re-freeze. Remove to a refrigerator about 20 minutes before serving. Serve with cream.

A sorbet can be made with the same ingredients, but with some extra edge from orange juice and more fresh mint.

RHUBARB AND STRAWBERRY SORBET

450 g / 1 lb rhubarb
225 g / 8 oz castor sugar
2 tsp vanilla extract
120 ml / 4 fl oz water
225 g / 8 oz strawberries, hulled and sliced
175 ml / 6 fl oz orange juice
1 tbsp fresh mint, chopped

Trim and slice the rhubarb, cook gently with the sugar, vanilla and water. Purée in a blender until smooth. Reserve. Blend the strawberries and the orange juice until smooth. Combine with the rhubarb. Chill. Make the sorbet in a machine, or by freezing in trays. When the freezing process is underway, stir in the mint and continue freezing.

RHUBARB AND GINGER ICE-CREAM

Rhubarb and ginger is the classic combination and works superlatively in an ice. There are many routes to happiness, and I will mention alternatives in the method which follows.

175 ml / 6 fl. oz orange juice
85 g / 3 oz granulated sugar
700 g / 1½ lb young rhubarb
15 g / ½ oz stem ginger
300 ml / 10 fl oz natural yoghurt

Measure orange juice into a stainless steel saucepan. Add the sugar, heat to dissolve, then bring to the boil. Peel the rhubarb, cut up finely, and poach in the syrup with the ginger for 8–10 minutes. Liquidize, rub through a fine sieve and cool.

Blend in the yoghurt and freeze in a metal container for 60 minutes. At this point, whip or stir the ice to break up any crystallization, then return to the freezer and whisk every 20 minutes until quite firm. On the other hand, you may be sufficiently equipped to merely put it in your ice-cream maker. It is better if not eaten straight out of the freezing compartment, but allowed to warm a little in the refrigerator.

A variation suggested by the late Marika Hanbury-Tenison was to sharpen the flavour with the addition of lemon juice and make the texture more interesting with the grated rind of an orange. Rather than using yoghurt, she proposed double cream and the white of an egg.

Some prefer ice-cream made with a custard rather than cream alone. Quantities for such a thing might read like this:

700 g / 1½ lb rhubarb, wiped, trimmed and cut up
120 ml / 4 fl oz water
125 g / 4 oz granulated sugar
225 ml / 8 fl oz milk
225 ml / 8 fl oz whipping cream
4 knobs of crystallized ginger, chopped

Cook the rhubarb with the water until tender. Sieve and reserve. Whisk the eggs and the sugar together in a bowl until they are lightened in colour and slightly thickened. Heat the milk and cream together in a pan until just on the boil, then pour on to the egg and sugar mixture, whisking all the while. Bring back to the stove (you may prefer to do this in a bowl set on a saucepan of boiling water) and whisk or stir until the custard is thickening, enough to coat the back of a spoon. Do not let it boil or the eggs will scramble. Leave to cool, then stir in the rhubarb and the chopped ginger. Chill.

At this point you may use your ice-cream maker, or you will want to freeze it in stages, bringing it out to stir and remove the ice crystals at intervals.

CHAPTER EIGHT

JAMS AND CHUTNEYS

Without Real Jam – cash and kisses – this world is a
bitterish pill.

Punch, 3 January 1885

The best jams are home-made. The shelves of shops are full
of factory produced jams, stiff with preservatives and artificial
setting agents. If you must buy it from a shop, buy it from
Oxfam. In bed-and-breakfasts and hotels they nonchalantly
dole out packlets of commercially produced marmalade and
strawberry jam. Wrestling with them adds a misery to even
excellent breakfasts. Making jam is not difficult, but it helps to
have an experienced friend to help you the first time.

First, assemble your equipment: you need a stainless steel
or enamel preserving pan or pan about three times as large as
the volume of fruit and sugar. You need a large bowl in which
the fruit and sugar can be placed overnight so that the sugar
becomes steeped in the juice which comes out of the rhubarb.
You will need to assemble more jars than you expect to use.
Wash them thoroughly and sterilize them by placing them in
the oven at about 150°C. You will also need jam-jar tops and
rubber bands. These can be bought in the same pack, together
with labels and wax discs.

Follow the directions for making your jam, stirring it
carefully until the sugar is completely dissolved, and then
from time to time. Skim off any froth, and when it becomes
transparent and starts to make heavy gluggy noises you can
start testing it for a set. Put a small amount on a cold saucer
and put it in the fridge for two or three minutes. While you
are testing it, remove the jam from the heat. Then see if the
sample wrinkles when you push the edge with a fingertip. If
it does not, then put the pan back on the fire and continue

cooking it. Alternatively, you may have a sugar thermometer. The jam setting temperature is 104°C/220°F. Many people use the thermometer as their guide but still do the refrigerator-wrinkle test as braces to the instrument's belt.

Now fill your jars nearly to the brim. I use a wide-mouthed funnel for this. While the jam is hot, wipe off any drips with a sterile, damp cloth. Cover the jam. First insert the waxed disc, with the waxed side hugging the surface of the jam. This must be done while the jam is either hot or cold, but never luke-warm. Take the transparent cover, moisten one side, and stretch it over the top, wet side uppermost. Secure it by stretching a rubber band over the rim of the jar. Allow the jam to cool, remove any surplus jam from the outside of the jars, and when they are dry, label them and store in a cool dry place.

I find that, generally speaking, cane sugar works better in jams and marmalades than does beet sugar.

As a rule, the small sticks of the spring crop, or the tender sticks of forced rhubarb, are not the best thing to use for jam. Make it after June, when the plant has some vigour and is possibly less filled with water.

In the pantheon of fruits, rhubarb is reckoned to be low in pectin, the magic factor that makes a jam or jelly set better. Some people take preventative action by composing a recipe that includes a high-pectin ingredient such as gooseberries or crab apples. Others ensure that they have included a citrus element. And a certain generation delights in adding pectin bought from the grocer or fudging it entirely by throwing in a packet of Jell-O. I have not found a problem with setting in the recipes I have used, low pectin or not.

Rhubarb and Ginger Jam

This is the commonest form in the north of Scotland. Here is the recipe as it was given me by the Shetland poet, Stella Sutherland of Bressay, in her own words, which have a vigour not usually found in recipes.

Equal parts of rhubarb and sugar. Preserved ginger chopped small (one ounce to 4 pounds) or ground cloves (one rounded teaspoon to 4 pounds).

Grease a pan well – bottom and well up the sides – use a large pan. Put in chopped, washed rhubarb and cover with the sugar. NO WATER. Leave the pan in a warm place, preferably on the outer, cooler end of a solid fuel stove till the sugar is dissolved. When the process is well advanced, stir it with a large wooden spoon, and when thoroughly dissolved, put it on the heat. Bring it to the boil, stirring constantly, and cook it for about an hour on reduced heat till it is a rich dark brown. (This cannot be achieved if the rhubarb is too young.) Keep stirring. Have jars hot and ready. Add flavouring and cook for only a few minutes. Pot and cover. It keeps almost indefinitely (if it gets the chance!)

Rhubarb Jam

Another Scottish recipe, this time from the kitchen notes of Lady Clark of Tillypronie, in which she acknowledges her source as Mrs Davidson from the Manse at Coldstone (just up the road).

This jam, which is marked "the older the better," is for roll puddings.

Cut the stalks of rhubarb in bits from 2 to 3 inches long; weigh them and put them in a jar with an equal weight of sugar; cover it with the sugar and let it lie some hours – use no water, as the rhubarb is so full of juice.

Put the jar in a pan of hot water to boil from ½ hour to 1 ½ hours according to whether the rhubarb is old or not; stir all the time; take it off to stand till cold. This is all.

But you can, if you like, add from the beginning a little ginger, broken roughly with a hammer and tied in a muslin to lie and cook with it, but remove the ginger later.

Something of the same simplicity is expressed by the vegetarian writer 'Domestica' (a Miss Baker) who wrote her *Vegetist's Dietary and Manual of Vegetable Cookery* in the 1870s.

The rhubarb must be young, and pulled in dry weather. Cut it in pieces about an inch long, (a silver knife is best). To 10 lbs rhubarb, add 1 oz powdered ginger, or the rind of 4 lemons shred or chopped fine; boil half an hour; then add 8 lb loaf sugar; boil three quarters of an hour.

Now for some jams using a wide variety of fresh ingredients. The next comes from the southernmost island of New Zealand. Stewart Island is separated from the South Island by a wind-swept and treacherous strait and, even in these days of air travel, contact with the wider world depends on wind and weather. Here you are very much in the Roaring Forties. From the air, the island appears to be entirely covered with bush, but there is a small settlement, Oban, with a little church out on a point. Here I found a small book of recipes sold for the church funds. Rhubarb grows well locally, but the amount of other fresh fruit available is fairly limited. It seems a strange paradox that in a place of such natural beauty factory-food should play a large part in the diet. Improvisation in such a situation is essential.

RHUBARB AND STRAWBERRY JAM (1)

I wouldn't make this jam if I had a wide choice of ingredients; it palls rather fast, but is very easy to make. It comes from that book I mentioned, on sale in the Oban Presbyterian Church, Stewart Island, in 1989. I have found similar recipes in books emanating from two other island communities, the Falklands and Shetland: in Tim Simpson's *Cooking the Falkland Island Way*, and in *The Church of Scotland Women's Guild Recipe Book: Shetland*.

5 heaped cups of finely cut rhubarb
5 cups of sugar
11 oz tin of crushed pineapple
2 packets of raspberry or strawberry jelly crystals

Place the rhubarb, sugar and pineapple in a large saucepan or boiler. Bring to the boil and boil for 10 minutes. Remove from the heat and let it cool slightly.

Add jelly crystals, stir to dissolve, and just bring to the boil again. Remove from the heat, cool a little, and pot.

RHUBARB AND STRAWBERRY JAM (2)

My source for this was *The New Home Cookery Book*, published by the Women's Institute at Levin, a town some miles north of Wellington in New Zealand. There are many versions of this recipe which deploy various setting agents, either gelatine or pectin. I do not find them necessary, but did add the juice of a lemon as some insurance.

1 kg / 2 lb rhubarb
1 kg / 2 lb strawberries
1.3 kg / 3 lb sugar
1 lemon

Slice the rhubarb quite small, roughly mash the strawberries; combine in a bowl; cover with half the sugar; macerate overnight. Place the fruit and the rest of the sugar in a saucepan and stir over a gentle heat until the sugar is dissolved. Add the juice of the lemon. Boil for 30 minutes. It set bang on the half-hour, just as the ladies said it would. Once tested for set, cool slightly, then pot up in sterilized jars.

RHUBARB, APPLE AND PASSION FRUIT JAM

I found the original of this in the French writer Christine Ferber's *Mes Confitures*, published in 2002. The passion fruit gives the jam a wild and exotic perfume.

450 g / 1 lb rhubarb
450 g / 1 lb apples
350 g / 12 oz granulated cane sugar for each 450 g / 1 lb of fruit
juice of a lemon
the pips, flesh and juice of 5 passion fruit

Rinse the rhubarb in cold water, cut the stalks in 5 cm / 2 inch lengths, then dice them. Peel the apples, quarter and core them, then slice finely. In one bowl place the rhubarb, 350 g / 12 oz of sugar and the juice of the lemon. In a second, place the apple, the juice and pips of the passion fruit and another 350 g / 12 oz of sugar. Cover each bowl and leave for an hour.

At this point, you can combine the contents of the two bowls, stir well and leave covered overnight. The next day, cook the mixtures in a heavy-based pan, stirring so the jam does not catch, and cooking until it reaches the correct temperature. Pot up and store.

A most excellent and similarly exotic recipe came my way when reading the New Zealand food-writer Gilian Painter's book *A Fruit Cookbook* (1984). She proposes a persimmon and rhubarb jam, given further perfume by adding either sweet cicely, angelica or lemon balm. This is the only modern author I have noticed using these old flavourings, most going for spices of some sort.

APRICOT AND RHUBARB JAM

I first tasted this at the Ben End, a tiny café overlooking Scalloway Harbour in Shetland, now sadly closed. It was run by sisters, relatives of Clement Williamson, the local photographer and author. It was not just the atmosphere of the Ben End which made their scones and jam memorable. It was the jam.

The recipe was given me by Anna Smith of the Ben End, but another version comes from Mrs Annie Thomson of Shirva, Fair Isle, who adds a few cloves in a muslin bag. This smells rich and spicy.

250 g / ½ lb dried apricots
150 ml / 5 fl oz water
675 g / 1 ½ lb rhubarb cut into 2 cm / ¾ inch lengths
sugar

Cut up the apricots finely, or mince, or process. Soak them overnight in the water. The next day, simmer them for 20 minutes. Then add the rhubarb and simmer gently a few minutes longer. Measure the mixture in a jug or with a cup before returning it to the pan. Measure out an equal volume of sugar and warm it in the oven. Add this to the fruit, and stir until dissolved. If the rhubarb is very mature, more water may be added to the fruit. Now cook the jam to setting point, pot up, cover and store.

The jam can be made with white or brown sugar. The brown makes it very different and characterful.

BLACKCURRANT AND RHUBARB JAM

The authors of the New Zealand recipe book *The Cook's Garden* are three sisters. They claim that this jam is preferred by their families to plain blackcurrant. For myself, I prefer the plain if there is double cream about for contrast; otherwise, I wouldn't quarrel.

675 g / 1 ½ lb rhubarb, finely sliced
675 g / 1 ½ lb blackcurrants, stalks removed
600 ml / 1 pint water
1.8 kg / 4 lb sugar

Cook the rhubarb to a pulp with half the water. Add the blackcurrants and the rest of the water. Boil for 20 minutes. Warm the sugar in a cool oven, then add it to the fruit and stir until dissolved. Boil rapidly about 15 minutes until the setting point is reached (see my notes at the outset of the chapter). Pour into warm sterilized jars and seal.

NANA'S RHUBARB AND BANANA JAM

This recipe came from the same three sisters and is found in their second instalment, *More from the Cook's Garden*, published a few years down the line.

1.3 kg / 3 lb rhubarb
1.3 kg / 3 lb sugar
75 ml / 3 fl oz lemon juice
4 large ripe bananas
1 tsp butter

Slice the rhubarb and combine it with the sugar and juice in a bowl. Leave 3 hours. Then put it in a jam pan and boil slowly for 30 minutes. Peel and slice the bananas and add to the boiling jam. Cook for 5 minutes more. Add the butter and skim. Pot.

CARROT AND RHUBARB JAM

1 kg / 2 ¼ lb sugar
450 g / 1 lb carrots
450 g / 1 lb rhubarb
the grated rind of 1 lemon and 1 orange
1 apple
1 tsp root ginger, finely chopped

Warm the sugar in a slow oven while busying yourself with the rest of ingredients. Wash and dry the carrots and rhubarb. Slice the rhubarb into 2.5 cm / 1 inch pieces, and grate the carrots. Combine in a large jam pan. Add the orange and lemon zest. Grate the apple and add it with the finely chopped ginger. Heat the pan gently, adding the sugar and stirring until the sugar is dissolved. Boil it until it reaches the correct temperature (104°C/220°F) and/or it sets when tested. Pot in sterilized jars.

GRAPEFRUIT AND RHUBARB JAM

My first encounter with this was through Pamela Westland's *A Taste of the Country* in 1976. Subsequently, many cooks have embraced it, not least in northern California where it seems to accord with the latest culinary fashion.

1.3 kg / 3 lb rhubarb, prepared weight
2 grapefruit & 1 lemon
1.3 kg / 3 lb cane sugar

Wash the rhubarb, trim it and slice it. Grate the rind off the grapefruit and lemon. Halve the surviving fruit and press through a sieve. Put the rhubarb, fruit pulp and peels in a basin and sprinkle with the sugar. Cover and let stand overnight. Transfer the fruit to a jam pan and bring slowly to the boil. Stir it often until it boils. When all the sugar is dissolved, boil it fast for about 15 minutes, and test for a set. Pot and cover.

Rhubarb and Gooseberry Jam

Jane Grigson was rather downbeat about rhubarb, the result she said, of an excess of rhubarb and custard in her youth. She made an exception, however, for this jam which figured in the great Victorian book about cookery in Wales, *The First Principles of Good Cookery Illustrated*, by Lady Llanover (1867). The recipe was given her ladyship 'by the venerable Mrs. Faulkener, of Tenby, South Wales, aged ninety-three, for many years landlady of the principal hotel there (*then* the White Lion).'

> Boil an equal quantity of rhubarb cut up, and gooseberries before they are *quite ripe*, with three-quarters of a pound of crystallized moist sugar to one pound of fruit. When boiled, it will make an excellent jam, similar to apricot.
>
> It will keep some time in a cool, dry place, tied down as usual.

Theodora FitzGibbon adjusted the recipe for modern readers in her *Taste of Wales* and added her own twist by including the heads of elderflowers, which should coincide with the first pick of gooseberries. Heady indeed.

1.8 kg / 4 lb rhubarb
1.8 kg / 4 lb green gooseberries
2.75 kg / 6 lb sugar
6 heads of elderflowers

Top and tail gooseberries, wash and wipe the rhubarb, and slice into small pieces. Put in a saucepan with the sugar, and then nearly cover with water. Bring to the boil, then boil rapidly for half an hour or until setting point is reached. Just before the jam is ready, infuse it with the perfume of elderflower by plunging the heads, wrapped in a muslin, into the boiling mixture. After the set has been reached, leave the jam in the pan for 10 minutes, then discard the elderflower. Pot up in the usual way.

Rhubarb, Lemon and Geranium Preserve

This recipe was given to Alice B. Toklas by Redvers and Louise Taylor of Bishops Lydeard in Somerset and included in her inimitable *Cookbook*, first published in 1954.

> 6 lbs rhubarb, 6 lbs sugar and 6 large lemons. Cut the rhubarb in small pieces. Slice the lemons very thin. Put the fruit in a large bowl and cover with the sugar. Let stand until it has drawn out the juice. Then boil for about ¾ hour. Do not stir more than necessary as its great beauty is in its not being all broken up. Place the leaf of a scented geranium in the bottom of each jar before bottling.

Rhubarb Marmalade

There are recipes which suggest making a marmalade with a texture similar to a coarse-cut, chunky Oxford marmalade. For instance, one idea is that you wait until the end of the rhubarb season, when the stalks are much drier. About 6 lb of them are cut into thin marmalade-like strips and mixed with the rinds of 3 lemons similarly sliced. Allow 1 lb sugar per lb of rhubarb, and half a pound for each lemon. Macerate the fruit and sugar for a day and a night then put to boil, adding the lemon juice last thing when the setting point is reached. I have also seen it advised that you make a muslin parcel of the pips and pith of the lemon to encourage the set.

The recipe here is for something simpler, or more delicate.

1 kg / 2 lb young rhubarb
750 g / 1 ½ lb sugar
grated rind and juice of a lemon or an orange

Chop the rhubarb finely and put in a basin with the sugar, rind and juice overnight. Stir to dissolve the sugar. Strain off the liquid and boil for 10–15 minutes to reduce it. Add the rhubarb and bring it to the boil again. Boil until the setting point is reached. Pot in the usual way.

RHUBARB JAM IN THREE DIFFERENT WAYS

This recipe comes from a book published on Shetland, at Lerwick, by Margaret Stout, called *Cookery for Northern Wives*. Perhaps she offered the alternative flavourings in case the right stores were not on the island when the cook needed to start jam-making.

2.75 kg / 6 lb rhubarb
2.75 kg / 6 lb sugar
1 cup water
2 lemons
   or 450 g / 1 lb dried figs
   or 60 g / 2 oz root ginger

Wash and dry the rhubarb. Slice into 1 cm / ½ inch pieces. Put in a basin or crock, add sugar and one cup of water to start the juice flowing, and leave for 24 hours. Put all into a preserving pan, and stir from time to time while coming to the boil. Slice the ginger into small pieces and add. Alternatively grate the lemon rind and add with the lemon juice or add the figs (which should have been soaked overnight then cut into small pieces). Boil the jam about half an hour until thick and jellied. Test, if need be, for set. Pour into warm pots. Cover when cold. The jam will keep for at least a year.

There is a recipe for rhubarb and fig jam in a little book produced by the Criccieth (South Wales) Women's Institute in about 1919. It was brought back to public attention by the Welsh food historian Bobby Freeman in a pamphlet called *Lloyd George's Favourite Dishes*. The instructions are of an eloquent brevity.

RHUBARB AND FIG JAM

6 lbs rhubarb, 5 lbs sugar, 8 oz [dried] figs, candied peel.
Cut figs and peel very fine, put over rhubarb with sugar
over night. Boil one and half hour.

Miss Griffith, Brynderwen

RHUBARB, ORANGE AND ALMOND JAM

The late Mrs E.A. Davies, a stalwart of the Women's Institute
and the Parish Council of Welshampton in Shropshire, gave me
this recipe many years ago, before she moved to live with her
daughter. She lived to be over 106. Until she was in her eighties,
every Christmas a cake arrived from her, topped with almonds.
They were the best Christmas cakes I have ever tasted.

1.8 kg / 4 lb rhubarb, peeled and cut into ½ inch lengths
1.8 kg / 4 lb sugar
4 oranges
2 lemons
225 g / 8 oz flaked almonds

Grate the rind of the oranges and lemons. Combine
in a basin with the rhubarb, and the citrus juice and
pulp. Add the sugar, and leave it 24 hours, turning it
over occasionally until the sugar is dissolved. The next
morning, in a heavy jam pan, boil quickly until the juice
is transparent and the peel cooked. Add the flaked
almonds and cook 5 minutes longer. Check for set; pot
and cover.

Rhubarb and Pineapple Conserve

In Felicity and Roald Dahl's amusing memoir, *Memories with Food at Gypsy House*, Phoebe Cavanagh contributes the suggestion for this excellent jam.

1 pineapple
1.4 kg / 3 lb rhubarb, cut small
juice and grated rind of 2 oranges
1.4 kg / 3 lb sugar
175 g / 6 oz flaked almonds

Peel the pineapple, remove its core and chop finely or put through a food processor. Add the rhubarb, the juice and grated rind of oranges and the sugar. Leave covered in a large bowl for at least 4 hours, or overnight. Then put in a jam pan and heat slowly, while stirring, till the sugar dissolves. Then cook rapidly till thick and clear. Check for set. Add the almonds and let it cool a little. Put into hot, sterilized jars.

Rhubarb Conserve with Dates and Raisins

I found this in a pamphlet put out by the Economics Division of the Department of Agriculture and Marketing, in Truro, Nova Scotia: yet further confirmation that rhubarb thrives in cool northern climes. I have retained the original North American quantities.

6 cups finely chopped rhubarb
2 tbsp water
1 cup granulated sugar
1 cup brown sugar
225 g / ½ lb dates, finely chopped
1 cup raisins

Put the rhubarb and the sugar in a large pan over a low heat and cook slowly till the rhubarb is tender. Add the dates and raisins and cook. Stir often until the ingredients are well combined into a soft mixture. This will take almost an hour. Pour into hot, sterilized jars and cover.

WALNUT, RAISIN AND RHUBARB JAM

1.8 kg / 4 lb rhubarb
walnuts as desired
1 orange
340–450 g / 12–16 oz seeded raisins
1.8 kg / 4 lb sugar

Slice the rhubarb fine and cook it in a little water in a heavy-based jam pan. Mince or process the walnuts, orange and raisins. Add them to the rhubarb, together with the sugar. Cook gently, while stirring, until the sugar is dissolved, then increase the heat and cook until it reaches the setting temperature (do not forget to stir from time to time) or until it sets according to the refrigerator test. Pot up.

Roslyn Presbyterian Church Jubilee Cook Book 1951

RHUBARB JELLY

Rhubarb doesn't just make premier wobbly jellies, of the sort I have described in an earlier chapter, but it is a fine and delicate jelly for spreading, and will set without assistance from gelatine or other agent.

young champagne rhubarb
cane sugar

Wipe and slice a quantity of nicely pink rhubarb. Cook it in a preserving pan with a smidgeon of water. Simmer until it has let out all its juice. Put it through a jelly bag and measure the final product. Allow 450 g / 1 lb sugar to each 600 ml / 1 pint of juice. Mix the sugar and juice together, cook steadily until the sugar is dissolved, then boil quickly until set is achieved (104°C/220°F).

This can be made into a savoury jelly by flavouring it with mint or with rosemary. Both go well with lamb, for example.

There are perhaps as many savoury rhubarb chutneys and relishes now in circulation as jams and conserves. This is a modern development, old recipe books do not have nearly so many. One that I did encounter in New Zealand was in the manuscript notes of a lady named Helen Wilkinson.

RHUBARB CHUTNEY

1 kg / 2 lb rhubarb, cut fine
775 g / 1 ¾ lb sugar
1 clove of garlic, cut fine
450 g / 1 lb sultanas
25 g / 1 oz salt
1 oz root ginger (bruised and put in a muslin bag)
300 ml / 1 pint malt vinegar
2 lemons, cut fine

Combine the ingredients and boil together slowly for 2 ½ hours or longer. Before potting, remove the ginger.

SPICED RHUBARB

1.4 kg / 3 lb rhubarb, washed, peeled and cut small
600 ml / 1 pint white wine or cider vinegar
450 g / 1 lb demerara sugar
1 tsp each ground allspice, ginger, cloves, cinnamon
½ tsp ground nutmeg
1 tsp salt

Prepare the rhubarb and simmer with a drop or two of water until tender. Boil the vinegar with the sugar, spices and seasoning. Add to the rhubarb, mix well and boil gently until thick. Pot.

The methods used in making chutney are similar to those for jam. Care must be taken that preserving pans and saucepans are made of enamel or stainless steel. Screw-top jars must be used with some sort of plastic, ceresin or cork lining. I simply re-use commercial chutney and jam jars, which always have suitable lids.

CHAPTER NINE

RHUBARB DRINKS

One day when my husband and I had a cottage in Shropshire, we were leaning over a bridge spanning the canal. It was a lovely evening and we weren't the only ones. An old man who lived nearby said to us, 'Come and see my little house'. So we went. By the back door he opened the door to the toilet with a flourish and solemnly flushed it. We were suitably impressed. Water had just come to the village. Then he invited us in for a glass of his rhubarb wine. There were three large casks. 'This one,' he said, 'we are drinking now. That's for next year, and that's for my funeral. It's going to be the merriest funeral in Shropshire!'

RHUBARB WINE

This mysterious recipe from the Orkney island of Westray was sent to *The Orcadian* in 1987 by a baffled reader. It brings a breath of the sea from a sea-girt island in a more remote time.

10 lb rhubarb
6 lb sugar
7 pence worth isinglass
7 pence worth burnt sugar [caramel]
2 Scotch pints of water [3 imperial pints]

Mash rhubarb with two large stones from the shore. Put it in the water, and leave it for 8–9 days, turning it every day. Add burnt sugar, isinglass and sugar, and stir thoroughly. Stir it each day until the scum stops rising. Then bottle and keep for five years before drinking.

According to the reader, the recipe was 40 years old. How much, he wondered, would sevenpence-worth of isinglass and sevenpence-worth of burnt sugar cost at today's prices.

Another recipe, which I found tipped into a cookery book from the early years of the last century, is quite sound and clear in its instructions.

To make 3 gallons of wine, use 14 lbs of rhubarb. Put in pan and bruise well. Pour on 3 gallons of cold water; add 3 lbs of sugar and 1 lemon cut in slices. Stand for 9 days, stirring each day, then strain off and add 4 lbs more sugar and 1 oz of isinglass put in bag to clear in 2 or 3 days time. Bottle off after a month or 2. Put in 2 or 3 lumps of sugar to each bottle.

Isinglass is used to fine or clarify the wine, it is the swim bladder of fish, often sturgeon. The idea that you put lump sugar into the bottles would seem to indicate a wish to provoke secondary fermentation in the bottle, i.e. bubbles. This idea of rhubarb wine being a competitor for champagne was taken up by a contributor to that great Victorian miscellany *Notes & Queries* in 1856. At the time, the French were suffering from powdery mildew or oidium which had infected the vineyards after contact with American stocks. This was a precursor to the devastation from phylloxera. A remedy for oidium was to administer sulphur. The following letter, headed 'Rhubarb Champagne' was sent by one J. Bruce Neil. It can scarcely have improved Anglo-French relations:

Can any of your readers inform me if any of the above wine is made in France? A few years ago, in 1852 or 1853, the French and English papers were loud in their praises of the above discovery; adding that it was equal, if not superior, to all other champagnes, and moreover it had the advantage, that it could be retailed at fourpence a bottle! Now I strongly suspect that more than half the champagne (owing to the failure of the grape crops, and the vine disease) imported into this country and sent to

America, is made from rhubarb; and I should like to be enlightened on the subject by some of our continental tourists and residents, as well as by all honest wine merchants. At the same time, perhaps, some of your informants will be kind enough to send you the recipe and directions, if the wine is (as I fancy it is) made in France, in order that we may try our hand at it in this country.

Recently, I have found an excellent sparkling drink from Normandy produced by the cider-maker Gérard Maeyaert. Nectar de Rhubarbe is slightly sweet, has less than 1 per cent alcohol, and makes the heat of summer days evaporate in a trice. This can only improve Anglo-French relations.

RHUBARB WINE

A more modern set of instructions comes from the practical book compiled by Dorothy Wise, *Home-made Country Wines*, published by *The Farmers' Weekly* in 1955.

2.25 kg / 5 lb rhubarb, cut up
4.7 litres / 1 gallon of water
225 g / ½ lb raisins
1 lemon
1.6 kg / 3 ½ lb sugar
20 g / ¾ oz fresh yeast

Place the rhubarb in a large bowl and pour 1 gallon of cool water over it. Leave it for 5 or 6 days, stirring it every day. Strain it through a muslin and then squeeze it as dry as you can. Chop the raisins and add them to the strained juice together with the thinly peeled rind of the lemon and its juice. Add the sugar. Stir it well and warm it gently until luke-warm, just so as to dissolve the sugar. Dissolve the yeast in some of the warm liquid and stir it in as well. Put it back into the bowl, or some other large (and very clean) vessel, cover it with three layers of clean cotton material, and leave for 24 hours in a warm place.

It can then be put into a fermentation jar with an air-lock for 2–3 months. During this period, rack it 2–3 times, and when fermentation ceases bottle it.

Note: Do not make after June, as the rhubarb becomes too tough and bitter.

RHUBARB VODKA

The taste for flavoured vodkas is addictive. Although many are impossible to make yourself, or best bought from proper Russian or Polish sources, a rhubarb- or fruit-flavoured spirit is quite within the bounds of domestic possibility. There are two ways of proceeding: either macerate the fruit with sugar, then add the spirit; or cook the fruit, before maturing the pulp in the vodka.

300 g / 12 oz rhubarb, chopped
120 g / 4 oz sugar
60 ml / 2 fl oz water
1 litre vodka

Cook the rhubarb with the sugar and water until tender. Put in a large glass storage jar or bowl. Cool. Add the vodka and cover. Store for about a week. Strain the vodka off the fruit pulp and bottle. Leave to mature for a bit.

Were you to do this by the maceration method, omit the water; find a 2-litre plastic bottle; cut the rhubarb small and insert it in the bottle. Use a funnel to add the sugar, screw on the lid and shake about to spread it around. Add the vodka. Store it in a dark place for 3 weeks or more, turning the bottle over every day or three. Strain off the vodka through a muslin and store in a tightly sealed bottle in the cellar for 3 months or more.

I have also read of a third method where the rhubarb is first left to macerate in vodka for a week. Then the spirit is strained off and stored separately while the rhubarb is mixed with sugar and stored in a sealed glass jar for 1 month. Then the contents of the two containers are combined and mixed thoroughly before being strained a second time. The spirit is now stored in the cellar for 3 months or more.

Some people spice up the simple flavour by adding lemon zest, cloves and cinnamon.

RHUBARB AND APPLE DRINK

I am grateful to Rosa Steppanova of Tresta on Shetland for this suggestion.

225 g / ½ lb rhubarb, sliced into 2.5 cm / 1 inch pieces
150 g / 8 oz apples, sliced finely
100 g / 4 oz strawberries
 or 1 carrot, grated
sugar to taste
orange juice (optional)

Liquidize everything together and, if it seems too thick, dilute with some orange juice. Chill, and serve at once.

BIBLIOGRAPHY

All books are published in London unless otherwise stated

Eliza Acton 1845, *Modern Cookery for Private Families* (Longman, Brown, Green, and Longmans; facsimile edition 1966, Paul Elek).

Anon. 1951, *Roslyn Presbyterian Church Jubilee Cook Book* (Dunedin, New Zealand).

Anon. 1987, *Fetlar's Favourite Recipes* (Fetlar Community Enterprises, Fetlar, Shetland).

Anon. 1989, *A Taste of the Falklands Islands* (Falkland Islands, Port Stanley).

J.H. Appleby 1982, ' "Rhubarb" Mounsey and the Surinam Toad – A Scottish Physician-Naturalist in Russia', *Archives of Natural History* 11 (1982).

Ursula Aylmer and Carolyn McCrum 1995, *Oxford Food, an Anthology* (Oxford University Press).

Annie A. Barnett 1915, *The Penlee Recipe Book* (G. Bell & Sons).

Isabella Beeton 1861, *Mrs Beeton's Book of Household Management* (S.O. Beeton; facsimile edition, Chancellor Press, 1982) .

Annie Bell 2006, *Gorgeous Cakes* (Kyle Cathie).

J. Bell of Antermony, *A Journey from St Petersburg to Pekin, 1719–22*, ed. J. L. Stevenson (Edinburgh University Press, 1965).

Mary Browne, Helen Leach and Nancy Titchbourne 1980, *The Cook's Garden: for Cooks who Garden and Gardeners who Cook* (Wellington, New Zealand, A. H. and A. W. Reed).

Mary Browne, Helen Leach and Nancy Titchbourne 1987, *More from the Cook's Garden* (Auckland, Reid Methuen).

Sally Butcher 2007, *Persia in Peckham* (Totnes, Prospect Books).

May Byron 1917, *May Byron's Pudding Book* (Hodder & Stoughton).

May Byron n.d., *May Byron's Jam Book* (Hodder & Stoughton).

Giacomo Castelvetro [1614], *The Fruit, Herbs and Vegetables of Italy*, translated and edited by Gillian Riley (Viking 1989; Totnes, Prospect Books, forthcoming).

Margaret Costa 1977, *Food for our Times* (Oxfam).

Felicity and Roald Dahl 1991, *Memories with Food at Gypsy House* (Viking).

William Darlington 1849, *Memorials of John Bartram and Humphry Marshall: with notices of their botanical contemporaries* (Philadelphia PA, Lindsay & Blakiston).

Erasmus Darwin 1800, *Phytologia...* (Dublin, P. Byrne).

Alan Davidson 2003, *North Atlantic Seafood* (Totnes: Prospect Books; first published by Macmillan, 1979).

Arto der Haroutunian 1982, *Middle Eastern Cookery* (Century).

Evelyn M. DeNike 1964, *Rhubarb for All Occasions* (Michigan).

L. W. Dillwyn 1843, ed., *Hortus Collinsonianus: an Account of the Plants Cultivated by the late Peter Collinson esq., FRS* (Swansea, for the Editor).

Josceline Dimbleby 1979, *Book of Puddings, Desserts and Savouries* (Harmondsworth, Penguin).

Dioscorides [1934], *The Greek Herbal of Dioscorides, illustrated by a Byzantine, AD 512...,* ed. John Gunter (Oxford, printed by John Johnson for the editor, Oxford).

George Dodd 1856, *The Food of London* (Longman, Brown, Green & Longmans).

Mistress Margaret Dods 1826, *The Cook and Housewife's Manual* (Edinburgh).

'Domestica' (Miss Baker) 1881, *The Vegetist's Dietary and Manual of Vegetable Cookery* (Tweedie and Co., 4th edition).

Christine Ferber 2002, *Mes Confitures* (Paris, Editions Payot & Rivages).

Theodora FitzGibbon 1974, *A Taste of Wales* (Pan Books).

Walter and Jenny Fleiss 1968, *Modern Vegetarian Cookery* (Harmondsworth, Penguin).

Clifford M. Foust 1992, *Rhubarb: The Wondrous Drug* (Princeton NJ, Princeton University Press).

Charles Elmé Francatelli 1852, *A Plain Cookery Book for the Working Classes* (Routledge, Warne, and Routledge; facsimile edition, Scolar Press, 1977).

Christine France 1985, 'Rhubarb, Rhubarb, Rhubarb', *Women's Realm* (April, 1985).

Bobby Freeman 1974, ed., *Lloyd George's Favourite Dishes* (Cardiff, John Jones).

Catherine Frances Frere 1909, editor and arranger, *The Cookery Book of Lady Clark of Tillypronie* (Constable; a new edition, with an introduction by Geraldene Holt, Southover Press, Lewes, 1994).

Olive. M. Geddes 1994, *The Laird's Kitchen* (Edinburgh, The National Library of Scotland).

Amanda Goodfellow 1989, *A Household Legacy* (Saffron Walden, Brewhouse Traditional & Wholefood Company).

Geoffrey Grigson 1955, *The Englishman's Flora* (J.M. Dent & Son).

Jane Grigson 1982, *Jane Grigson's Fruit Book* (Michael Joseph).

Nathalie Hambro 1981, *Particular Delights* (Jill Norman and Hobhouse).

Rosemary Hemphill 1966, *The Penguin Book of Herbs and Spices* (Harmondsworth, Penguin).

Mrs Annabella P. Hill 1867, *Mrs. Hill's New Cook Book* (New York, James O'Kane; facsimile edition of the 1872 edition of G.W. Carleton, New York, by University of South Carolina Press, 1995).

William Kitchiner 1829, *The Cook's Oracle; containing receipts for plain cookery,...* (Cadell & Co., Edinburgh; Simpkin & Marshall, and G.B. Whittaker, London; and John Cumming, Dublin; the first edition was published in 1817).

Jessica Kuper 1977, ed., *The Anthropologist's Cookbook* (Routledge) .

Cornelis le Bruin 1737, *Travels into Muscovy, Persia, and part of the East Indies ... Translated from the original French* (A. Bettesworth and others, London, 2 vol.; originally published in Dutch in Amsterdam in 1711, translated into French in 1718).

Lady Llanover 1867, *The First Principles of Good Cookery Illustrated* (Richard Bentley; a facsimile edition, edited by Bobby Freeman, was published by Brefi Press, Tregaron, Dyfed, 1991).

Doris Janzen Longacre 1987, *More-with-Less Cookbook* (first published in the USA in 1976; English edition, Tring, Lion Paperbacks).

Roberta Longstaff, and Dr Jim Mann 1986, *The Healthy Heart Diet* Book (Martin Dunitz).

Richard Mabey 1996, *Flora Britannica* (Sinclair-Stevenson).

Claire Macdonald (Lady Macdonald of Macdonald) 1983, *Seasonal Cooking from the Isle of Skye* (Century).

Fred Macnicol 1978, *Hungarian Cookery* (Alan Lane).

Jenny Mann 1982, *Vegetarian Cuisine* (Fontana).

Mrs A.B. Marshall 1894, *Fancy Ices* (Marshall's School of Cookery; a facsimile reprint was published by Liz Seeber, Lewes, Sussex, in 1999).

Mrs A.B. Marshall n.d., *The Book of Ices* (Marshall's School of Cookery).

Henry Mayhew 1861, *London Labour & London Poor*, volume 1 (Griffin, Bohn).

Philip Miller 1732, *The Gardener's Dictionary* (Dublin edition).

Joyce Molyneux with Sophie Grigson 1990, *The Carved Angel Cookery Book* (Collins).

New Covent Garden Soup Company 1999, *New Covent Garden Soup Company's Soup and Beyond: Soups, Beans and Other Things* (Macmillan).

New Zealand Country Women's Institute, Levin 1956, *The New Home Cookery Book*.

Marja Ochorowicz-Monatowa 1958, *Polish Cookery* (first published in Polish in 1910, an adapted English translation by Jean Karsvina published in America by Crown International and in London by Andre Deutsch).

Henry Phillips 1822, *History of Cultivated Vegetables* (H. Colburn and Co.).

Cathy Prange and Joan Pauli 1982, *Muffin Mania* (Kitchener, Ontario).

Claudia Roden 1985, *A New Book of Middle Eastern Food* (Viking).

Maxime Rodinson, A.J. Arberry and Charles Perry 2001, *Medieval Arab Cookery* (Totnes, Prospect Books).

Helen Saberi 2000, *Noshe Djan, Afghan Food and Cookery* (revised edition, Totnes, Prospect Books).

Roger Scola 1992, *Feeding the Victorian City: The Food Supply of Manchester 1770–1870* (Manchester, Manchester University Press).

George and Cecilia Scurfield 1963, *Home-made Cakes and Biscuits* (Faber & Faber; a recent edition has been published by Serif, 1993; and more recently still by Grub Street, as *Home Baked, A Little Book of Bread, Cake and Biscuit Recipes*, 2009).

Tim Simpson 1994, *Cooking the Falkland Island Way* (Bangor, Peregrine Publishing).

Catherine Sinclair 1840, *Shetland and the Shetlanders or The Northern Circuit* (Edinburgh, William White and Co. Ltd.).

Henry Southgate 1874, *Things a Lady Would Like to Know* (Edinburgh, Walter Nimmo).

Catherine Stott 1984, *The Best of Marika Hanbury-Tenison* (The Daily Telegraph).

Margaret B. Stout 1925, *Cookery for Northern Wives* (Lerwick, T. and J. Manson).

Lydia Strong 2004, *St. Andrew's Recipe Book* (Penrith) .

Alice B. Toklas 1954, *The Alice B. Toklas Cookbook* (New York, Harper & Bros.; a current English edition is published by Serif, London).

John Tovey 1992, *The Miller Howe Cook Book* (The Ebury Press).

Caroline Waldegrave, Puff Fairclough, and Janey Orr 1995, *Leith's Easy Dinners* (Bloomsbury).

Pamela Westland 1976, *A Taste of the Country* (Harmondsworth, Penguin).

C. Anne Wilson 1973, *Food & Drink in Britain from the Stone Age to Recent Times* (Constable).

Dorothy Wise 1955, ed., *Home-made Country Wines* (Countrywise Books published by *The Farmers' Weekly*).

Websites

http://www.mysteriousbritain.co.uk/scotland/dumfriesshire/hauntings/rammerscales-mansion.html [for James Mounsey]

http://www.yorkshirerhubarb.co.uk/ruhbarb_triangle.htm

http://www.morleyarchives.ik.com/p_rhubarb.ikml

http://www.glallotments.btik.com/p_Rhubarb_Triangle.ikml

http://www.motherlindas.com/rhubarb_reminiscences.htm

http://www.rhubarbinfo.com/
[*The Rhubarb Compendium*, virtually everything you need to know about rhubarb, how to grow it and how to cook it.]

http://www.brandycarrnurseries.co.uk/company/history.htm

http://www.thomasjeffersonpapers.org [for Thomas Jefferson's Garden Book]

http://www.madohg.org.uk (Millom and District Oral History Group)

INDEX OF RECIPES

Given the subject of the book, the name rhubarb is not itself indexed.